Denver's Elitch Gardens

Elitch's Zoological Gardens

Denver, Colo.

Denver's Elitch Gardens

Spinning a Century of Dreams

Betty Lynne Hull

Johnson Books

BOULDER

Published by Johnson Books, a division of Johnson Publishing Company, 1880 South 57th Court, Boulder, Colorado 80301. Visit our website at www.JohnsonBooks.com. E-mail: books@jpcolorado.com.

9 8 7 6 5 4 3 2 1

Cover design by Debra B. Topping
Cover photos courtesy of the Gurtler family

Library of Congress Cataloging-in-Publication Data
Hull, Betty Lynne, 1944–
    Denver's Elitch Gardens: spinning a century of dreams / Betty Lynne Hull.
        p. cm.
Includes bibliographical references and index.
    ISBN 1-55566-285-4
    1. Elitch Gardens (Denver, Colo.)—History. I. Title.
    GV1853.3.C62D467 2003
    791.06'87883—dc21   2002156659

Printed in the United States by
Johnson Printing
1880 South 57th Court
Boulder, Colorado 80301

Printed on ECF paper with soy ink

To Jim for his support,
To Sandy Gurtler for sharing family stories,
And to the Gurtler family for the historic photographs.

Contents

Mary Elitch
"The Gracious Lady of the Gardens"

1

Into the Gay Nineties

IT WAS 1880, a magical time—reflected in the glare of the Gilded Age—aglow with the effects of the Industrial Revolution. Railroads served as the conduit for the nation's desire for urbanization as a steady torrent of people flooded westward with their hopes in their satchels or on their backs, oblivious to the few disheartened forty-niners trickling back from California, their pockets filled only with deflated dreams.

Those fragile hopes were now centered in the young state of Colorado, whose wild frontier days had ended with the coming of those same railroads. Now these mighty locomotives served a new master—mining. Trains rumbled constantly through Denver's recently completed Union Station, and new towns sprang up almost daily throughout the ore-rich mountains. The world's largest silver nugget, 93 percent pure and weighing over a ton, had just been found in Aspen's Smuggler Mine.

The East may have had its Vanderbilts, awash in scandal and flaunted wealth, but Colorado reveled in its own version of wealthy decadence—in the person of silver magnate H.A.W. Tabor, who had deserted his staid and proper wife, Augusta, for a beautiful blonde divorcée half his age. He had recently lodged her in the fanciest suite of Denver's newly built elegant hotel, the Windsor, and dared anyone to tell him nay. His good friend, Fred Pitkin, was Colorado's governor, and pals Henry Teller and Nathaniel Hill represented the state in Congress. After a stint in Colorado as lieutenant governor, Tabor would briefly join them in Washington, D.C., with a thirty-day senatorial term, duly bought and paid for.

And all the while, the silver flowed like water—$11 million worth in 1880 alone.

Back in 1859, John Gregory had discovered gold in nearby Clear Creek and the cry of "Pikes Peak or Bust" had brought thousands of disillusioned farmers, starving European immigrants, and land speculators, all in search of riches. With them came gamblers, runaway slaves, and fancy ladies. Disputes were settled with bullets, and punishment was efficiently dealt with a rope.

Little Montana City, St. Charles Town, rough Highland Town, Fountain City, El Dorado, and busy Arapahoe grew up all along the South Platte River and Cherry Creek. Auraria, under the direction of Dr. Levi Russell, was one of the largest of these small settlements. It served the area as the cradle of pioneer business life, with a well-attended church and Owen Goldrick's school, as well as William Byers's daily paper, *The Rocky Mountain News*. Auraria's rival was bawdy Denver, run by William Larimer, whose primary boast was the existence of thirty successful saloons.

All of these separate settlements soon saw the advantage of becoming united, and the Municipality of Denver was formed in April 1860, and incorporated in November 1861. The new town had a population of one thousand lodged in over 160 buildings, some adobe or log and some frame, all of them unpainted. Wooden sidewalks teemed with men and women, while the rutted, dusty streets were filled with oxen pulling massive freight wagons and strings of laden mules bound for the mines.

Life wasn't easy—the necessities were costly and in short supply. Coffee, beans, pork, bread, and whiskey each cost over a dollar, twice what a skilled prospector could make in a day.

In 1862, President James Buchanan signed a bill creating the Colorado Territory and appointed William Gilpin as its first territorial governor. Shortly thereafter, a woman named Martha Hagar arrived in the Territory with her husband and sons. This frontier family settled in the mountain town of Empire, which served as a food distribution center for the local Ute Indians. Unfortunately, some drunken renegades butchered her husband one dark night, so Martha moved her sons to the safety of Denver, where she met and married William Chilcott. He talked her into homesteading a farm five miles to the west of the town. The land contained good water and a small lake, and Martha soon planted numerous trees—cottonwoods for shade and an apple orchard for taste.

By the time Colorado had been admitted as a state in 1876, Denver, under the guidance of Mayor Richard Sopris, already bore an air of prominence, even though it still served as the jumping-off place for the fabulous silver and gold deposits in the mountains. And by 1880, not unlike New York's Park Avenue, the city boasted of its own "Millionaires' Row" along Grant Street. Developer Henry C. Brown created an elite residential area on the gentle hills adjacent to the State Capitol, which was called "Brown's Bluff." The mansions on Brown's Bluff sported crystal chandeliers, leaded glass windows by Tiffany, tapestried walls, statuary, turrets, and towers, and belonged to such men as Governor John Evans, Senator Nathaniel Hill, railroader David Moffat, and cattle baron John Iliff.

That winter, the Ute Indians were forcibly moved to a vast reservation that would eventually become Utah. After all, their homeland was needed for farming and cattle ranching, and Denverites were now much too sophisticated to bother themselves with the welfare of mere savages. Why, the good people of Denver could now brag that they enjoyed all the culture and amenities of the big cities of the East!

In fact, several amusement parks had opened and enjoyed immediate popularity. The first of these was called River Front Park. It was located on the eastern side of the South Platte River and extended between 15th and 19th Streets, bounded on the east by busy Union Station. It had been built by John Brisben Walker who, in addition to other business endeavors, was the publisher of *Cosmopolitan* magazine. The park contained an oval racetrack and grandstands, a gymnasium, tennis courts, a skating rink, a toboggan run, a bandstand, a canoeing and boating channel, and a baseball diamond. Walker even dammed up the Platte to form a berth for his steamboat, which he used as a casino. He loved fireworks and held spectacular demonstrations of them every weekend.

River Front Park hosted Buffalo Bill's Wild West Show and P. T. Barnum's circus. At about the same time, Arlington Park opened along Cherry Creek at Corona and East 4th Avenue. It was renowned for its trained animal acts and the small boats that were sent down narrow

Denver ⁓ *c. 1880*

chutes into a lake at the bottom, creating a sort of early-day water theme park.

One afternoon in 1880, another young couple stepped off the train from San Francisco. Their names were John and Mary Elitch, and like so many others, they had come to Colorado to seek their fortune. They were as unlikely a couple as anyone could imagine. John, six years older than his wife, was a large man, athletic and well muscled with a ready smile and a bluff manner. His wife, on the other hand, was petite and sweetly demure.

John had been born in 1850 in Mobile, Alabama. He was quite proud that his mother was a descendant of Alabama's Stephen Hopkins, a signer of the Declaration of Independence, and that his father was a

John & Mary Elitch ⌒ c. 1890

decorated officer in the Confederate army. He had grown up under the hardships of the South's Reconstruction and had moved to San Francisco as soon as he was able to leave home. There, jobs were easy to come by for a young fellow who wasn't afraid of honest labor. He soon found his niche working in restaurants in the city's theater district. He was drawn to the magical world of the theater and enjoyed the occasional acting job.

One fateful day in 1872, he met a shy, sixteen-year-old convent-schooled girl named Mary Elizabeth Hauck, who lived in San Francisco with her parents. She would later say that John's charm and love of life had "overwhelmed her" and "swept her off her feet." They eloped to

San Jose, where John took his excited young bride to her very first play, *The Streets of New York*, starring Frank Mayo. The newlyweds returned to furnished rooms in San Francisco and John's new job as the manager of the popular Mannings Oyster Grotto.

But they dreamed the dreams of all young couples, and John believed Denver was rife with opportunity. So they carefully counted their savings, packed their meager belongings, and boarded the train to their destiny.

One of the first things they witnessed upon their arrival in the new town was the brutal cleaning out of Denver's "Hop Alley." This was an area between Blake and Market around 20th Street that housed five hundred local Chinese, most of whom were workers left behind from the construction of the Transcontinental Railroad. As they watched the mounted police set torches to the crowded shacks, John tried to explain the realities of racial inequities to his shocked, tender-hearted wife.

Before the week was out, John had found a job in the busy Arcade Restaurant on Larimer near 16th Street. And before a year had passed, a surprised Mary learned that her husband had purchased what would soon be called The Elitch Palace Dining Room, located at 1541 Arapahoe Street. John was proud that it contained one of the longest bars in Denver. The restaurant was an immediate success. In addition to becoming a regular stop for road-weary travelers and work-weary miners alike, it was a favorite of the locals, including John's friend, newspaper reporter Eugene Field.

It wasn't long before John could refer to some of Denver's most influential men as friends—men like Senator H.A.W. Tabor, Mayor Wolff Londoner, railroader David Moffat, Governors John Evans and

The Elitch Palace Dining Room

John Routt, newspaperman Thomas Patterson, and the up-and-coming William Stapleton. With them, he helped organize the Denver Athletic Club.

Mary was happy with their life these days. Her interests included gardening and painting. In fact, she was president of the prestigious Denver Art Club for a time. John teased her about being so soft-hearted—she was always taking in stray dogs and cats. She was disappointed that children hadn't come to them, but overall, she was content. Just when she thought they were well settled in their little rented cottage, one day in 1888 John told her that he had purchased the sixteen-acre Chilcott Farm in the Highlands northwest of Denver. He assured her it was a sensible buy, emphasizing all the money they

The former Chilcott Farm & the future Elitch's Zoological Gardens

would save by growing their own produce for their restaurant. He needn't have worried. Mary fell in love with the farm as soon as she saw it. She would later write, "The Highlands were something of a wilderness, for few streets were in common use. Mr. Elitch and I would take the buggy from the gates of our ranch diagonally across the plains and down the hill, across the Platte River into Denver. A visit to 'the City' was a day's event to us."

She loved the shady coolness of her green oasis and the acres of space. Her every spare moment was spent planting, weeding, and otherwise tending her flowers, and soon the farm fairly blossomed from every available nook and cranny. She had also recently expanded their little family. P. T. Barnum, a family friend, had given Mary some surplus baby circus animals, as had Harry Tammen, the new owner of the Sells-Floto Circus, which wintered on the shores of nearby Sloan's Lake.

One sunny afternoon a year later, as she and John strolled in the apple orchard, he mused aloud how much their farm reminded him of the lush, green loveliness of San Francisco's famous Woodward Gardens. This was a popular playground for families that neither tolerated "rough company" nor sold any liquor on the premises. San Francisco's women and children often spent their day there with propriety.

Mary listened to her husband carefully. By now she had been married to John long enough to tell that another change in their lives was in the wind, and she dreaded it. She wasn't wrong; a concept that would completely alter their simple farm had indeed been born.

2

A Dream Is Born

ELITCH'S ZOOLOGICAL GARDENS OPENED MAY 1, 1890, in a profusion of apple blossoms and pouring rain. But even the rain couldn't dampen the couple's excitement. All their hard work was about to pay off. John had built zoo enclosures for Mary's animals, and she had designed acres of walkways and fountains amid her lush flower beds. There were benches and picnic tables placed at comfortable intervals under the big cottonwoods, and a gazebo-shaped band shell, crowned with a carved lyre, beckoned atop a gentle slope. John had planned a vaudeville performance under a tent as the highlight of the day. He had long dreamed of building a magnificent theater on the grounds and spent a great deal of that winter designing it with the help of the local architectural firm of Leiden & Lee. It would be crowned by a dome modeled after Shakespeare's famous Globe Theatre, and the painted canvas curtain he had ordered would also follow a Shakespearean theme. (That painted canvas curtain, decorated with Anne Hathaway's cottage, is still intact in the venerable old theater today, over a century later.)

Unfortunately, he barely had time to begin construction on his theater before the Gardens' opening day. His goal was to bring quality entertainment to Denver. "Just wait until next season," he promised himself eagerly. He would make his theater the talk of the entire country! He basked in the image of himself as theater manager, director, and star.

According to Mary Elitch's letters, she shivered when she woke up that morning. There was no turning back now. John had sold their restaurant. The new owners had immediately renamed it Tortoni's. (It would remain a popular Denver nightspot for another thirty years until Prohibition finally closed it down.)

To help them celebrate the Gardens' opening, John had invited his friend P. T. Barnum, who in turn brought *his* friends, Mr. and Mrs. Tom Thumb. John also invited several other old friends who thought enough of him to journey all the way from San Francisco to be there for his greatest triumph—famous comedian Nat Goodwin and thespians May Irwin and James O'Neill, father of playwright Eugene O'Neill.

Mayor Wolff Londoner had planned to give a welcoming speech at the rough-hewn log entrance gate, but he was drowned out by the fanfare of several trumpeters as the gates swung open to admit the considerable crowd. So he saved his words until later in the vaudeville tent.

"Ladies and Gentlemen," he began as the rain pattered on the canvas over his head, "Denver has been longing for a place where a working man and his family can come and spend the day … where no lady will be offended by any disorderly person," and the vaudeville performance commenced. It was a full bill of fare. There were the Montgomerys, comedians, sketch artists, and banjoists; Bailey & Reynolds, who specialized in comedy, singing, and dancing; comedian Charles

Elitch Gardens entrance gate ᵀ 1890–1908

Goodyear, an Elitch friend; Van Auken & La Van, who were horizontal bar performers; the lovely Bijou Mignon who sang and danced; Charles Schilling, another Elitch friend, who was billed as a musical comedy genius; Rosa Lee, a ballad specialist; and acrobats Ed Nealy & John Sully. The talented Zola family closed the program.

During the afternoon, the sun finally peeked through, encouraging guests to stroll along the shaded pathways, pausing to admire Mary's fountains and flower beds as they listened to the music of Peter Satriano and his band playing merry tunes from the gazebo-shaped band shell. An admirer, Edouard Hesselberg, later that summer composed "Elitch's March" in tribute to the couple's creation. John had it played daily during that first season and gave copies of the sheet music as souvenirs. Hungry diners crowded into the just-completed Orchard Café or

Site of Elitch Gardens' afternoon band concerts

clustered under the trees around overflowing picnic baskets. A soda fountain booth and a confectionery pavilion nearby offered libations and sweet desserts.

Mary, still childless, had a special spot in her heart for children and planned a large portion of the Gardens for their enjoyment. There were, of course, swings, slides, and teeter-totters, but also pony rides and carts pulled by her pet goats. The first children's picnic was given in June of that inaugural season. It was sponsored by J. S. Appel Company, and all of Denver's Sunday school children were invited.

Mary's zoo was a favorite stop for all. Guests delightedly watched lions, camels, buffalo, deer, elk, and bears, one of whom stood up and

The Orchard Café ☞ *1890–1980*

waltzed to the band music. Mary even kept a mischievous ostrich who snatched the buttons off the children's high-button shoes and pulled his mistress around the grounds in a cart.

P. T. Barnum enthusiastically congratulated John on his zoo, and before the day was out, the two men had composed a letter to the famous importer, Forepaugh, to place a standing order for rare and unusual creatures.

The final activity of opening day was a baseball game on John's athletic field. He joined several local luminaries in the game as the sun disappeared behind the mountains. Eugene Field ably covered the entire day for the *Denver Republican* newspaper.

*To the delight of her guests, Mary Elitch's pet ostrich
pulled her around the Park in a small cart*

Mary Elitch with some of her "babies"
☞ c. 1893

Mary Elitch with a gift from her friend P. T. Barnum

Elitch's Zoological Gardens was two miles beyond the nearest street-car line, so John hired horse-drawn trolleys to bring guests to the entrance gate. He was already in negotiation with the West End Electric Car Company to run a line directly to the Gardens, but it wouldn't be operational until the following spring.

John and Mary's first season was a tremendous success. They had grossed an unbelievable $35,000 by the time the gates closed on Labor Day 1890. They were tired but very, very happy. John had found his lifework and Mary was content to help. She was surrounded by her flowers, her animals, and an abundance of happy children. She told a newspaper writer, "We maintain the highest standards of family enter-

Busy Elitch Gardens at the turn of the century

tainment. We allow no public dancing, no liquor and no raucous criers ballyhooing some tawdry show." Her life was complete.

That winter, John grew restless and decided to form the Goodyear, Elitch, and Schilling Minstrels with two old friends. He planned to tour the Pacific Coast to earn extra money. He returned home for Christmas and left again soon after. In February, Mary was urgently summoned to the Melville House in San Francisco. John had fallen ill with pneumonia and was asking for her. A mere three weeks later, on March 10, 1890, he was dead. Devastated, Mary made arrangements to accompany his body back to Denver. During the long journey she couldn't keep from thinking how different this trip was from the first she and John had made over those same rails eleven years before. Was it really eleven? It seemed like yesterday.

Mary buried her husband at Denver's Fairmont Cemetery. She erected a large, ornate tombstone adorned by John's bust. Eventually, she would be laid to rest beside him.

She spent the next months deciding what to do. Ever since the day she had met him, John had made their decisions. She felt lost. Her family wrote to her, urging her to return to San Francisco. But after the exciting and unpredictable life she had led with John for the last eighteen years, that option threatened to suffocate her. Simply put, he had opened her eyes and shown her the world's possibilities. He had always had such a joy of life.

Finally, she knew what to do. "I determined to make these Gardens famous as a memorial to my husband," she would write years later. "My husband's death left our Gardens in my inexperienced hands. Our great adventure was still something of an experiment. I decided to undertake the management of the place myself, and so for the next twenty-six years, I operated the resort alone. It was a heavy burden."

From the start, however, she proved to have a flair for the spectacular. One of her newspaper advertisements for the 1891 season read:

Come see the bears stand up and beg for peanuts; the monkeys slide down their toboggan slides, and the fierce billy goat engage in deadly conflict with the sacred bull of India (actually an elderly water buffalo named Kelly). And the baby lions—why, they're a whole zoological park in themselves. Come gaze in wonder at Mac, the largest lion in captivity. Come feed the buffalo, camels and the herds of deer and elk who wander about the Gardens.

Mary Elizabeth Hauck Elitch ≈ 1892

But the greatest achievement that season was the completion and opening of John's theater (originally called the Playhouse in the Gardens and later renamed the Theatre at the Gardens). It featured both vaudeville and light opera that summer.

A rival amusement park, Manhattan Beach, opened that year on the north shore of Sloan's Lake at what would become 25th Avenue and Sheridan Boulevard, bringing even more pleasure seekers to the Highlands west of town. Manhattan Beach became known primarily for its beach bathing, swimming, and boating, but the park complex also contained a large theater or auditorium, built for dancing and entertainments. The owners soon realized they lacked the expertise to bring in any such talent, and wisely hired Mary to manage their theater as well as her own. She enlisted the aid of John's old friend, Charles Schilling, who had recently married her little sister, Anna. Together they successfully comanaged both endeavors for several years.

The silver panic of 1893 devastated the entire West, and certainly Colorado. In fact, nearly one-third of Denver's population suddenly found itself unemployed. Mary's Gardens, however, enjoyed record crowds. Perhaps a day at her amusement park provided a needed escape for the people of Denver.

Elitch's Zoological Gardens' first major attraction, Thomas Edison's Vitascope, was presented for the 1896 season. It was an enlarged Kinescope, and projected images onto a screen for all to see. Sophisticated Denverites were enthralled and flocked to view the city's first moving pictures, bragging that they were the first to be made available in all of the western United States. The subjects were as varied as they were exciting—everything from a passion play to scenes fresh from the battlefields of Cuba (1898). Actually, the Spanish-American War had elicited a great deal of local patriotism. For its part, Elitch's Zoological Gardens featured elaborate floral displays in the shapes of intertwined American and Cuban flags.

The 1897 season was noteworthy for several reasons. The first of these was Mary's hiring of local daredevil Ivy Baldwin with his ascension balloon dubbed "The Aerostat." The balloon was huge—65 feet in diameter, 200 feet in circumference, involving 5 miles of rope and 8,840 yards of silk over a basket made of seasoned willow reeds. The gas-filled orb would rise, tethered, to a terrifying height of 1,500 feet offering breathless patrons a spectacular view of the surrounding countryside.

To celebrate the Fourth of July that year, Baldwin planned to jump from his balloon at sunset with lit fireworks attached to his back. His asbestos suit didn't arrive in time, but he jumped anyway and was subsequently feted for his bravery. He would complete nearly five thousand such jumps in his decade-long tenure at the Park. And it wasn't long before *the* place to hold one's wedding was the ascension balloon at Mary Elitch's Gardens.

The year 1897 was also when Mary began a seventy-year tradition of summer stock theater, presenting a challenging ten-week season offering ten different plays. Her first leading man was the renowned thespian James O'Neill. He had known John in San Francisco and was now honoring a promise he'd made. "I'll come back and play on that stage whenever you say," he had said.

George Edeson became the first of a long distinguished list of capable directors. Jane Kenmark was chosen to be the first leading lady of "the Theatre at the Gardens." The plays offered that first season included

Ivy Baldwin,
balloonist extraordinaire

Ballooning was a popular pastime
at Elitch Gardens in 1897

Helene, *Fool of Fortune*, *The Rajah*, and *A Bachelor's Romance*. Mary was quite proud that she paid her actors salaries equal to those offered in New York.

The Elitch Gardens Orchestra (actually Denver's first symphony orchestra), led by Signor Cavallo, brought the famous Paderewski to town in 1897. The Gardens' Friday afternoon concerts were *the* place to see and be seen for Denver's society matrons. Signor Cavallo would be replaced fifteen years later by the popular Harold Tureman.

The Zoo at the Gardens continued to be a very popular and increasingly famous attraction. In 1898, a London newspaper referred to Mary's zoological collection as "the finest west of Chicago." Rex, one of the zoo's lions, was such a magnificent specimen that he was used as the model for the marble lions that still grace the entrance of the Chicago Art Institute. When Ed, one of her favorite lions, died, Mary had a taxidermist create a rug from his skin and head, which remained on the floor of her bungalow until her death. Years later, in preparation for Elitch Gardens' fortieth-anniversary celebration in 1930, Denver residents were asked to submit their memories of the early years at the Park. Miss Anna Herpick wrote:

> When I was a child a severe illness left me totally blind. My father took me to Elitch's Gardens and gave me the opportunity to examine every tree, flower and shrub in it. I loved these things when I had my sight and I wanted to touch them and see them once more in my own way.
>
> We were standing in the apple orchard when I asked Father to lift me up so I could touch the fruit. Before he could do so, Mrs. Elitch, in the course of her daily walk around the grounds, approached and told me to pluck all the apples my father could hold in his pockets.
>
> Intuitively, I knew she loved children, and when Father placed me on the ground, I clung to her hand and begged her to show me the animals

in her zoo. When we came to a lion, Mrs. Elitch offered to let me stroke his head. However, Father wouldn't allow it. I never quite got over the disappointment of being denied this wonderful experience.

Last summer, a number of us who are blind, attended a performance at the Theatre. Afterwards, Mrs. Elitch invited us into her home for refreshments and to examine the souvenirs she had collected over the years. There, on the floor was the skin of that wonderful old lion. Mrs. Elitch said the lion had been a family pet and one of the finest specimens she had ever seen.

Now I could sit on the floor and stroke his noble head just as much as I pleased.

Sam and Dewey were Mary's favorite black bears, and she made great pets of both of them. Each evening the two hairy beasts would be released from the bear pit and would lumber past startled visitors on their way to Mary's cottage. There, they would stand on their hind legs and beg to be admitted. Mary would do so with great ceremony. They would then follow her into her kitchen where she would feed them treats. One day while Mary was gone, little Dewey got out of the bear pit on his own and broke the cottage's windows as he pounded on them to be let in. He cut his paws so badly on the broken glass that he bled to death before his mistress returned. Everyone dreaded having to tell Mary what had happened.

Sam took a great liking to the actor Fredrick Perry, and much to the great man's horror, followed him adoringly around the park. One evening, the petrified thespian was rescued by Park employees who spied him desperately grasping the fence a full three feet off the ground as he gingerly edged his way along the far side of the baseball field in order to avoid the bear.

Mary Elitch with her favorite bear, Sam

Mary's zoo was one of the few to have seals born into captivity. In May 1898, she held a contest in the local papers to name the new babies, but was never thrilled with the names "Celia" and "Cellina" that were chosen. One of Mary's favorite monkeys, Dude, escaped one busy afternoon while his cage was being cleaned. He ran into the theater and completely disrupted a dress rehearsal. Jess, one of Mary's elephants, often was put to work clearing tree stumps and even moving small buildings. Usually, one of the maintenance people would walk ahead of him offering a bag of peanuts as motivation.

After the Gardens closed for the season, the deer, elk, buffalo, ponies, and other tame animals were given the run of the property for the winter. Sometimes, things got out of hand. Mary wrote:

Mary Elitch enjoying her bears
➣ *c. 1895*

"The Theatre at the Gardens" ⋍ *c. 1891*

I was called away suddenly to the bedside of a sick friend and neglected to close the house. When I returned, I beheld a sight I'll never forget. Three deer, an elk and an ostrich were in my home. The ostrich was in the kitchen knocking pans and dishes all over the room. The elk was in the pantry. She had found a large jar of jam and had smeared it all over the wall, floor, shelves and herself. One deer lay on my bed and the other two were roaming about the parlor. They had upset some vases of flowers and water was spilled all over.

Charles and Anna Schilling told Mary they planned to move back to California before the onset of the 1899 season. Now she would be completely on her own. In the end, she made the decision to not only keep her Gardens going, but to also expand and improve the Park for the new century. She had learned that the city planned to increase public

A busy theater matinee ⌒ c. 1898

transportation outside the Park's gate from a single horse-drawn trolley to three electric lines. To Mary, this signaled the promise of a new era. She made the difficult decision to incorporate, and subsequently sold stock at $1 per share. With the amazing $300,000 she raised, she built a small electric plant that provided increased electrical lighting throughout the Park, new stone zoo buildings, more elaborate landscaping, a penny arcade, and also construction of a popular "Historic Reenactment." It was called "The Naval Spectacle," and enacted the battle between the *Monitor* and the *Merrimac*, and later, the sinking

Mary Elitch at her bungalow ⌁ c. 1897

of the *Titanic*. (In 1910, Mary would construct a new modern building with the very latest mechanical and electrical effects on an enormous stage, complete with elaborate sets involving full-size ships and real guns. Unfortunately, in 1914 the building was destroyed by a fierce fire that nearly took the entire Park, and it was never rebuilt.) Mary used the remainder of the money to increase the budget for her theater, mostly going for salaries and to hire a manager, Thomas Long.

Her improvements paid off. The 1899 season at Elitch's Zoological Gardens was a memorable one, especially in the theater. Mary selected

Mary Elitch rows on the lake in the southwest corner of her Gardens

Walter Bellows as her director. Her leading man that season was Howard Hansel, and her leading lady was Henrietta Crossman, a major star. Plays would include *Trilby*, which had been a sensation in New York the previous year; *Svengali*; *Charity Ball*; *The Senator*; and *Cyrano de Bergerac*, which required a cast of over one hundred locals. Rehearsals were made up of an amazing mixture of professionals and amateurs. The talented Bellows successfully blended this enormous crowd of people into a smoothly functioning company. And suddenly, most of Denver was in love with the dramatic arts.

As the old century ended, Mary had gained the distinction of being the only woman in the world to successfully own and manage a summer resort. She became known by all as "the Gracious Lady of the Gardens," a name given her by Frank White, a writer for the *Denver Post*. She set the tone of her Gardens as a clean, wholesome, family-oriented park, creating a philosophy that was always conscientiously followed and has persisted through the years. Interestingly enough, a man in California adopted that same philosophy in the mid-1950s as part of his concept for a major amusement park—his name was Walt Disney.

Years later Mary would write, "I have never spent a summer away from my Gardens, the picture I painted for all to enjoy. Every tree holds its own story for me; every flower its own memory."

Mary contentedly spent three to four months each winter in San Francisco and New York, attending plays and planning new attractions for her Gardens.

3

The Promise of a New Century

THE NEW CENTURY brought many changes to Denver. Millionaires had disappeared almost as fast as had the demand for their silver. It seemed, too, that Denverites were anxious to put their humble frontier roots far behind them. As the city grew, so did its ethnic prejudices. Like the rest of the nation, Denver had become a melting pot, and those poor souls at the bottom were, as usual, barely tolerated. These included the blacks, the Mexicans who toiled in the fields, and the Chinese house servants, janitors, and laborers. Above them were the Italians, many of whom worked in construction or in the mines, and finally the Jews, who tended toward careers in banking and medicine. All of these good people came, put down roots, and left their mark.

Then, in 1914, Denver found itself in the midst of an economic boom brought on by "the war to end all wars." Silver soared to $1 an ounce! The sons fought and bled, and those who didn't die came back home to a myriad of problems—inflation, unemployment, and labor unrest. Denver even had its own "Red Scare," which caused fear and hatred of Bolsheviks and all other foreigners. This was hardest on the influx of Polish refugees who had arrived at the end of the war and settled in the Globeville area.

Suddenly, there were loyalty oaths for teachers and support of national immigration legislation. The newly constructed "Welcome" arch at Union Station was a cruel travesty to many. And yet, the city had its good side too. The annual Festival of Mountain and Plain, begun in 1895, continued to be enormously popular. American Indians still danced in full regalia, businesses decorated floats for the parade down city streets, and costume balls were held all over town.

Colorado joined the rest of the country in Prohibition, but its citizens didn't suffer overly much since Wyoming, whose citizens chose not to participate, provided a steady flow of liquor all the while.

By the 1920s, the Ku Klux Klan was on the rise in Denver under the leadership of Grand Dragon Dr. John Galen Locke. As elsewhere, the Klan began as a benign fraternal organization dedicated to good works, but its anti-Catholic, anti-Jewish, anti-black philosophy soon corrupted any noble goals it may have had. Unfortunately, John Elitch's old friend, Ben Stapleton, now Denver's mayor, had close ties to the Klan. Soon Klansmen held nearly all appointive city offices.

And how fared Mary Elitch's Zoological Gardens in this new century? Very nicely, thank you. She had outlasted all her major competition. Arlington Park, renamed Chute City, closed in 1902; River Front Park closed in 1903 after John Brisben Walker sold off the land to the railroads; and popular Manhattan Beach, which had been renamed Luna Park in 1909, was gone by the outbreak of the war. Mary's only rival now was a small, family-owned amusement park located at 46th

Elitch Gardens' popular miniature railroad ~ *c. 1905*

Avenue and Sheridan Boulevard in what was then known as "White City." It opened in 1908 and was called Lakeside. Over ninety years later, these two amusement parks still enjoy a friendly rivalry.

In celebrating the new century, Mary married her manager, Thomas Long, in 1900, and the couple departed on an around-the-world honeymoon tour. Meanwhile, her Park flourished. A miniature train, which had taken two years to build, was ready on its 12-inch narrow-gauge track. The coal-burning engine weighed 450 pounds with a six-gallon water tank. Its boiler could achieve 175 pounds of pressure. The little train had eight cars and each held up to four children or two adults. Additionally, there were afternoon band and evening symphony concerts in the theater.

When the newlyweds returned, they formed the Elitch Long Management Company and opened a comic opera, *The Wizard of the Nile*, at nearby Manhattan Beach, which was still under Mary's management. It was so successful that they moved it to their own Theatre at the Gardens. That winter they, along with Walter Bellows, contracted to operate the Lafayette Square Theater in Washington, D.C.

On a visit to the famous Luna Park on New York's Coney Island, Mary tried out a "Figure 8" or Toboggan Coaster ride. She got in the car and it slowly pulled her up a long, narrow trestle to the top. Suddenly, it whirled down and around, up and around, and finally, with a floating motion, came to a slow stop. As Mary was helped from the little car, she straightened her large hat, laughed, and said, "Let's do it again!" Sure enough, Elitch's Zoological Gardens had its own Toboggan Coaster ride by opening day of the 1904 season.

The highlight of Mary's 1905 season was Dr. Carver's diving horse attraction and its stars, Powder Face and Cupid. To the delight of the crowd, they dived, with no urging, from a thirty-five-foot tower into a deep pool of water.

In 1906, a marvelous carousel, manufactured by the prestigious Philadelphia Toboggan Company, arrived. It carried beautifully hand-carved representatives of all the animals in Mary's zoo, along with graceful horses. There was a lion, a tiger, camels, deer, and zebras, as well as a mythological hippogriff. Mary had seen a similar merry-go-round at Manhattan Beach and knew she had to have one just like it to entertain her own visitors. A Wurlitzer Monster Military Band Organ provided accompanying music and had the instrumentation to equal a twelve- to fifteen-piece band. A portable, steam-driven merry-go-round

Mary Elitch's first carousel in her Gardens ⟶ *1906*

had been at Elitch Gardens for several years prior to this, but it was soon
sold off and forgotten in the splendor of this new masterpiece.

These early days at Mary's Gardens were captured in the memories
of its guests. These reminiscences, written in 1930, were in response to
a local newspaper's invitation to mark Elitch Gardens' fortieth anniversary, and are well worth revisiting.

Helen Foster wrote:

> I remember the day when most of Denver's population rushed out to
> Elitch Gardens to watch the spectacular ascent of Mr. Baldwin in his
> death-defying balloon.

Elitch Gardens' Toboggan 8 Coaster
◦ 1904

Guests smile atop the Toboggan 8 Coaster ◦ 1904

Those were the days when the Merry-Go-Round vied with the tiny, cinder-spitting miniature train for honors as Elitch's most exciting ride. No amount of hot cinders down my neck or blinding smoke in my eyes could ever dim its joy for me.

The zoo held a special interest for me at that time too. For in it, in the monkey cage, was one particularly wise old fellow whom I believed recognized me from season to season as an enemy because of a fatal mistake I made on my first visit to him. I unwrapped and ate a piece of luscious golden brown taffy in front of his cage without offering him a piece too. Seeing me, he became so enraged and insulted that he grabbed the bars of his cage and shook them until they rattled all the while screaming at the top of his lungs. He repeated this performance every time he saw me for years.

I don't remember too much about the Theatre in those early years. But I do remember attending Matinees with my Mother and sitting there primly in my best dress and my tightly braided pigtails and fanning my hot, flushed face with a palm-leaf fan that the management had passed around. I always wanted to take one of those fans home with me, but my Mother always made sure I returned it.

J. O. Lalor wrote:

Elitch Gardens? I remember ... horses and buggies, streetcars with side seats, and cars with colored lights. I remember seeing the first automobiles while walking home after spending my last nickel on the Merry-Go-Round.

Why doesn't fried chicken taste as good as it did under the old apple trees in the orchard? I remember wonderful flower gardens and sneaking in over the high board fence.

The first wild animals I ever saw or smelled were at Elitch's. That old zoo smell is still strong in my memory, as is that ostrich that pulled the cart. I wish I had all the peanuts I threw in the bear pit ...

You know, no airplane today gives the kick the old hot air balloons and parachute drops did. I wonder where all the folks are who got married in that balloon?

Elitch's was always respectable; you had to behave yourself. What wonderful stars have performed in the old Theatre … what glorious productions!

Estelle Stewart wrote:

Childhood and Elitch Gardens … what magic words—what memories they awaken!

An amusing incident of my childhood still lingers in my mind. One afternoon, I went to Elitch's with some other children for a picnic. We ate our lunch under some trees. Afterward, we strolled over to the zoo and the ostrich pen.

We had some hard-boiled eggs left over from our lunch and as children will, we decided to feed them to the ostriches. To our amazement, one of them swallowed an egg whole! My eyes grew wider and wider as I saw a great lump gradually descending his long neck. We were all frightened, fearing it would choke him to death, and like all mischievous children, we scampered away in a hurry.

And finally, from Mary Ross:

Elitch's—the "perfumed garden," sweet with not only a myriad of flowers, but also fragrant with memories of the famous ones who have strolled its paths.

Elitch's, where the whiffs of heliotrope waft on soft summer breezes or greet you in the shafts of sunlight glinting through the apple blossoms to shimmer on the lawn and rustic tables spread with a delicious picnic. Such good sandwiches, and oh, the fried chicken!

Then the moon comes up on the many colored lights glimmering fairy-like among the trees along the walks. The music pulses in the distance. You wander toward the Theatre greeting and chatting with friends …

The "Lady of the Gardens," whose guiding genius and unfailing ideals have made it a thing apart. Not once has its high standard been lowered or its bright, clear record tarnished.

Children's Day at Elitch Gardens, ballet class

Elitch's fame is not only local, but has even gone abroad. On an ocean liner bound for Paris, we were speaking of Denver when a foreigner remarked, "Oh, then you know Elitch Gardens; I have been there too."

In 1906, Thomas Long was killed in an automobile accident. Mary would never marry again. Her Gardens were her salvation and became the only remaining focus of her life.

In 1909, Mary's old friend, Maggie, "the Unsinkable Molly" Brown, cajoled into demonstrating something she had learned on one of her European sojourns, gave a memorable yodeling exhibition as part of the Gardens' Kindness to Animals benefit. This was only one of the charities and causes Mary Elitch supported in Denver. Residents of Denver's Old Ladies' Home were guests of the Gardens every Wednesday, and, of course, Tuesdays were Mary's famous Children's Days when all children were admitted free. Among them, she, too, could be a child again—so important since she had never been blessed with little ones of her own. A classical school of ballet was featured as well as ballroom and folk dancing lessons, animal study, elementary botany, dramatics, painting lessons, along with costume parties and contests. Mary led nature walks and sing-alongs. Local Ute Indians were hired to teach Indian lore and crafts. Mary made sure numerous prizes were given and everyone enjoyed themselves. The highlight of the afternoon was a formal tea hosted by Mary at her home with an emphasis on manners and deportment.

Dorothy Morgan wrote:

> One very hot day, I chanced to visit the Gardens when throngs of happy children played in the sunshine. Right in the middle was a beautiful elderly lady who laughingly greeted first one child by name, then another, and who resembled an ethereal being, almost a part of the sun-drenched blooms that so profusely decorated the grounds. I waited in awe as she was surrounded again and again.
>
> I found out later that this gracious hostess was the owner of Elitch Gardens. I never forgot that scene ... may that lovely Lady of Elitch's leave others memories like the one she gave me, a casual visitor to Elitch Gardens on Children's Day.

During these years, the Theatre at the Gardens flourished. Miss Blanche Bates arrived from New York for the 1901 season with no fewer than ten trunks of clothes. Plays that season included *Dancing Girl*, *Rosalind*, and *As You Like It*. For the latter, the rear wall of the theater was removed to extend the stage under the stars for more realistic

Popular Children's Day at Elitch Gardens

"The Theatre at the Gardens" ⌒ *1891–1991*

forest scenes. Miss Bates was such a hit that all of her performances were standing room only.

Mary completely remodeled the ten-year-old theater for the 1902 season. She had the stage widened, the boxes enlarged and redecorated, and the second-floor walkway enclosed.

Colorful Maude Fealy arrived fresh from the London stage for the 1903 summer stock season. She became a close friend of Mary's and appeared in the Elitch Gardens Theatre each summer from 1899 to 1905. One summer, Governor Peabody, an admirer, presented her with a

The interior of "the Theatre at the Gardens"

Elitch School of the Theatre ~ c. 1920

handsome silver loving cup on behalf of appreciative Colorado audiences. Maude Fealy would eventually settle in Denver and manage the Elitch School of Drama for local aspiring thespians.

This was also the season Henrietta Crossman shocked Denverites by speeding through downtown streets in her new horseless carriage. They shook their heads in disapproval, telling each other how wild those theater people were.

Antoinette Perry, after whom the famous Tony award is named, appeared on Mary's stage in 1904 at the age of eleven. She was billed opposite her father, the incomparable Fredrick Perry. May Buckley, who appeared each season from 1904 to 1908, was the leading lady that season.

The *Chicago Tribune* wrote, "While the rest of the country has been in the theatrical dumps, the City of Denver has been a bright spot on the map."

The 1905 season brought the young acting brothers William and Cecil B. DeMille. (Cecil B. DeMille would send a congratulatory telegram to the Elitch Gardens Theatre for each season's opening until his death, calling it "one of the cradles of American drama.") Walter Clarke Bellows had replaced George Edeson as director. One of the plays offered that season was *Tess of the D'Urbervilles* with Tyrone (Tom) Power, Sr., appearing in the lead role opposite his wife, Edith Crane. The couple also thrilled Denver audiences with their rendition of *The Taming of the Shrew*. (Their son, movie star Tyrone Power, would reprise his father's role on the silver screen years later. In his turn, Tyrone Power III would play the theater for the 1982 and 1983 seasons, continuing a proud Elitch Gardens tradition.)

It was in 1906 that Mary knew her theater had truly arrived. Sarah Bernhardt was scheduled to perform in San Francisco, but the theater there was destroyed in the earthquake. So she stopped at Elitch Gardens instead and, with her heavy French accent, performed in *Camille* in the afternoons and *La Sorcière* in the evenings. Local actors volunteered to work with her for no pay so they could forever after boast of appearing onstage with "the Divine Miss Sarah."

Miss Bernhardt enjoyed her time at Elitch Gardens, and was often seen around Denver in her trademark drooping black hat and heavy veil. She helped Mary feed the bears each afternoon, and with great ceremony, named a mountain lion kitten after herself.

Sarah's leading man was a local fellow named Douglas Fairbanks, who had hung around Elitch's theater since he was twelve years old, offering to sweep the stage in exchange for tickets. Maude Fealy had been his acting teacher in her Elitch School of the Theatre. One can be sure the theater quickly sold out for the rest of that summer season!

Claire Rafferty wrote:

> I remember when we attended the Theatre at Elitch Gardens many years ago. I have forgotten the exact date but I think it was David Warfield and Antoinette Perry in *The Music Master*.
>
> Everyone was enjoying the production when Mother Nature decided to outdo the performance on the stage. Mighty claps of thunder repeatedly drowned out the spoken lines. Flashes of lightning were occasionally visible, and here and there throughout the audience umbrellas appeared for those fortunate enough to have them since the old, leaky roof provided only scant protection against the damp.
>
> The sudden storm ceased, and was soon forgotten in the enjoyment of the play. But when the Theatre released its patrons, we all realized our troubles weren't over yet. We still had to get home. Wading through ankle-deep mud to the streetcar demonstrated a love of Elitch's that has never waned.

Other great stars to appear on the Elitch stage during those years were Spring Byington (1907, 1914–1916), George Arliss (1905–1906, 1913), Lewis Stone (1913), and finally, Harold Lloyd (1914), who had also grown up in Denver. Each season the actors autographed the old gray stage door. It was interesting to note that the more prominent the actor, the smaller and more obscure the signature. Years later, Mary, in an uncharacteristic show of temper, would fire the unfortunate employee who had painted over the door, not realizing its sentimental value.

In 1908, the hospitality of the Gardens was extended to the delegates to the Democratic National Convention being held in Denver. And in

SARAH BERNHARDT
AT ELITCH'S GARDENS

Elitch's

Mrs. MARY ELITCH LONG. Proprietor.

MATINEE THURSDAY, MAY 24, 1906

Farewell American Tour of the World's Greatest Actress

Madame Sarah Bernhardt

From the Theatre Sarah Bernhardt, Paris, and Her Own
Company
PRESENTING

"LA SORCIERE"

A Drama in Five Acts, by M. VICTORIEN SARDOU
Stage Music by M. XAVIER LEROUX

*Sarah Bernhardt, 1906,
leading lady in
Elitch Gardens' Theatre*

Douglas Fairbanks, Sr. 1906

1911, Mary instituted Parent/Teacher Day honoring the Denver schools. It began with a parade and featured students performing folk dances and plays. All proceeds were turned over to the Parent/Teacher Association, which at that time was under the direction of Mrs. Fred Dick. A local poet even celebrated the event in verse:

> *What changeful dream is this?*
> *For there be elves and fairies all about!*
> *No, they are children, Denver's own,*
> *Secure and happy, playing 'neath the trees,*
> *And yonder, to complete their joy, SHE comes,*
> *Their guardian queen—the Lady of the Gardens.*

In 1909, Mary decided to replace her old log entrance gate with an impressive and elaborate Greek Revival–style stucco edifice. But by this time Mary was having trouble keeping Elitch Gardens on sound financial footing. Running an enterprise as large as her Park had become was simply too much for her. She needed help.

She turned to John's old friend, Ben Stapleton, who in turn enlisted the aid of several prominent businessmen led by Hungarian Flour founder John Mullin. The men were afraid Mary would sell the Park to powerful F. G. Bonfils, who at that time held controlling interest in the Sells-Floto Circus. These businessmen decided to form a consortium to pay Mary's bills and bring her taxes up-to-date in exchange for stock. She was frantic when she realized she was losing control of her beloved Gardens and knew she had to do something, and quickly.

Elitch Gardens' stucco entrance gate ⌐ *c. 1909–1958*

4

The Beginning of a Dynasty

MARY ELITCH LONG had indeed lost control of her beloved Elitch Gardens. In effect, a consortium of Denver businessmen now owned the Park. They, however, had no desire to get caught up in the day-to-day operation of their new acquisition, so one of their members, Robert Speer, convinced his good friend, another respected businessman, John Mulvihill, to take over management for them.

John Mulvihill was born in 1869 in Dudley, Pennsylvania. He received a degree from Duff College in Pittsburgh and returned to Dudley to teach. After several years, he moved on to teach at the Pennsylvania Reformatory at Huntington. Following this, he was associated with the executive offices of Carnegie Steel in Pittsburgh. Mulvihill came to Colorado in 1902. His first job in Denver was with the Credit & Collections Department of the Denver Gas & Electric Company, and he was soon appointed as manager. Next, he ran for an available seat on the local school board, but, being Catholic, found himself on the wrong side of the influential local Ku Klux Klan. It was to no

John Mulvihill
President, Elitch Gardens
☞ 1916–1930

one's surprise that he lost. Family members often related the old family story of how Mulvihill shooed his wife and little daughter to the basement so they wouldn't see the cross burning on their front lawn.

One of the first and longest-enduring friendships John Mulvihill made was with Mayor Robert Speer. When the mayor came to him with the proposition to manage an amusement park and zoo, he agreed.

Within a few months, however, John Mulvihill knew he wanted to purchase the Park outright, and the consortium was pleased to recoup their investment so quickly. Mary, sensing his love for her precious Elitch Gardens, also gave her blessing. So, in 1916, the papers were signed.

There were three conditions that Mary placed on the sale. The first was that the name of the Park could never be changed; the second was that she could continue to live in her bungalow on the grounds until her death; and last, that the two lower boxes to the left of the stage in the theater would always be reserved for her friends and herself. This box contained fourteen seats, and it often overflowed with ladies dressed to the nines in silks, feather boas, and graceful pitcher hats, happily chatting away throughout the performances.

As the 1920s began, Mary continued to live at the Gardens, now free from the responsibilities of ownership, in a new, modern house that John Mulvihill had built for her on the grounds. Daily, she strolled among her flower beds, smiling and greeting guests just as she always had. Mary had a lifelong love of poetry and often quoted verses aloud from the beautifully illustrated volume of *The Rubaiyat of Omar Khayyam* that she carried. This was given to her as a wedding present by her husband, John. Mary spent the rest of her days surrounded by

The Wildcat Coaster ⌁ 1922–1994

friends, pets, flowers, and the treasured photographs of her "family"—the famous actors who had performed at her theater.

John Mulvihill immediately made some changes to Elitch Gardens. The first and most important of these was economic stability. In her later years, Mary had begun to pay the bills that arrived when she happened to have cash on hand, and to ignore the ones that came when she didn't. Mulvihill, on the other hand, quickly set up a long-overdue formal bookkeeping system. He also invested a considerable amount of money in acquiring new attractions that he hoped would provide something for everyone.

Elitch Gardens' Ferris wheel ⌒ 1936

The Old Mill Tunnel of Love ⌒ 1936

One of these attractions was the wildly successful, seventy-five-foot-high Wildcat roller coaster, first built in 1922 (and expanded in 1936). "Twist his tail and hear him roar!" read the newspaper advertisements of the day.

Another attraction was the Old Mill, which offered guests a slow, dreamy boat ride on a small canal through an enclosed "tunnel of love." It had first been built in 1914. Riders, when they felt the need to look beyond the face of their chosen partner, gazed upon lighted, life-sized tableaus of popular fairy tales that were placed in alcoves in the walls along the way. The ride was remodeled in 1928. Electrical conduit was installed, and the dangerous original knob and tube wiring removed.

Mulvihill added a popular haunted house attraction. He also greatly expanded the shaded picnic grounds, and improved the gourmet meals available at the Orchard Café. He had large, white-columned pergolas erected over the walkways to protect guests from passing summer showers as well as the heat of Colorado's summer sun. He engaged Rudolph Ganz to conduct a seventy-five-piece symphony for concerts every evening.

Arriving just in time for the 1928 season was the new carousel that Mulvihill purchased from the Philadelphia Toboggan Company, where Mary had purchased hers in 1906. In March 1927, he had placed an order for "a new, modern, elaborately carved 4-abreast carousel, highly ornamental and substantially built of good materials in a skilled, workmanlike manner and highly embellished with gold and aluminum leaf."

The factory shipped him a work of art that had taken the master craftsmen in Philadelphia nearly three years to carve by hand. John must have swallowed hard when he paid out a whopping $20,000 for

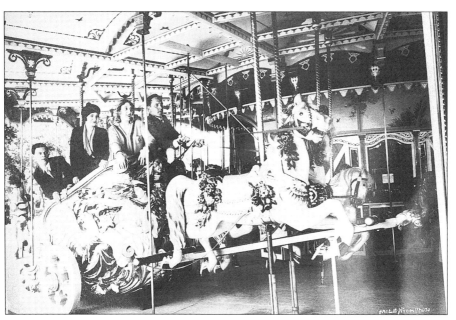

Actor Fredric March fancies himself as Ben-Hur aboard Elitch Gardens' carousel in 1928

Elitch Gardens' carousel ~ *1928*

the attraction. That same carousel, which still greets guests just within the gates of Six Flags Elitch Gardens over seventy-five years later, has recently been appraised at well over one hundred times that amount.

This marvelous new carousel featured sixty-four horses—forty-four jumpers (horses that went up and down as well as around), twenty large, outside row standers (stationary horses that just went around), and two impressive Roman-style chariots. All were carved from pieces of yellow poplar, laminated together and hollowed out for lightness. Nails and screws were seldom used; instead joints were pegged and glued together with animal-hide glue.

Because each carver was encouraged to use his imagination, each horse is different and unique: in the way it paws the ground, the magnificent arch of its neck, the impatient toss of its head, or the mischievous swish of its tail. This carousel was designated by the factory as "PTC #51." It is considered unusual in the carousel world because it contains carvings by three of the industry's most important carvers.

Frank Caretta carved most of the horses. His carvings are distinctive in that they are massive—almost boxy—and give the impression of power and strength. Every carousel has a lead horse, which is more elaborately carved than the others. On this machine, the lead horse resembles a knight's armored charger. It prances beneath flowing robes, its proudly tucked head crowned with a carved feather plume. Further, it has a rare signature—a stylized monogrammed "PTC" emblazoned on a shield on its shoulder.

John Zalar, known as the "Michelangelo of Carvers," carved the two large chariots and magnificent, realistic chariot horses. The first of these chariots, affectionately called "Angel," features a life-sized angel

complete with widespread wings, attended by cherubs draping a garland of roses across her flowing gown. The other chariot is known as "Columbia." A Lady Liberty figure wrapped in an American flag graces the front. She is seated below the bust of an American Indian complete with a feathered headdress.

The harnesses of these chariot horses are liberally decorated with roses, and a carved feather plume jauntily crowns each headstall. Additionally, the singletree on each chariot ends in an elaborately carved lion's head.

Some years ago, two small, inner row ponies—whose startlingly lifelike beauty had been hidden under many years of paint—were discov-

"Columbia"

ered to have been carved by Gustav Dentzel, who was regarded by the carousel industry as the "Master of all Carvers." When Gustav died, his son Bill took over his carving shop. Then, when Bill died in 1928, the Philadelphia Toboggan Company bought up all the remaining Dentzel stock. It is by pure luck that two of these priceless carvings were included at the last minute in the carousel John Mulvihill purchased.

The eighteen scenery panels were decorated with painted scenes and beveled mirrors, and the sheet-metal domed ceiling was painted to resemble a tranquil sky, complete with birds, butterflies, and clouds. Silver musician cherubs smiled benignly down upon those eagerly awaiting a ride.

Six Flags Elitch Gardens' carousel is a survivor of a truly endangered species. Fewer than two hundred now prance and gallop where there were once several thousand across the country. Unlike the ever-changing thrill rides, the popularity of an amusement park's carousel depends upon the visual beauty and magnetism of its uniquely hand-carved horses and the enchantment created in the imagination and memories of its riders. There is no difference between a carousel and a merry-go-round. Both go in a counterclockwise direction. Only a British roundabout travels clockwise. Also, the word "carousel" can be spelled several ways. At Elitch Gardens, it was always spelled "carrousel."

As automobiles began to replace the interurban trolley as transportation to the Park, John Mulvihill turned the original farm entrance on 38th Street into a new "automobile" gate, and razed several of the zoo buildings to make room for a parking lot. Reminiscent of John Elitch and his ideas, he sensed a great advertising tool in the making. So, with the cooperation of the Hover Motor Company, he began handing out spare tire covers decorated with the slogan "Not to See Elitch's is Not to See Denver." These words successfully advertised the Gardens for over fifty years and, in fact, still decorate the Ferris wheel at Six Flags Elitch Gardens today.

John Mulvihill expanded Mary's flower beds into acres of carefully tended formal gardens. The newspapers of the day called the Park "a flower-laden wonderland." He razed additional zoo buildings to build extensive greenhouses, which eventually would nurture tens of thousands of exotic blooms under 160,000 square feet of glass.

He was so successful in this endeavor that he branched into the flower business, and along with his young manager, Walter Lehrer,

Elitch Gardens turned the original Chilcott Farm entrance on 38th Avenue into an automobile gate

started the Elitch-Long Floral Company. Lehrer would later own Lehrer's Flowers, one of Denver's most successful floral enterprises.

Perhaps the greatest addition John Mulvihill made to Elitch Gardens, however, was the Trocadero Ballroom. Mary Elitch had always disapproved of public dancing, and must have raised an eyebrow in 1917 when it opened. The Trocadero name was borrowed from a popular southern California ballroom. It was finished in pale yellow stucco trimmed with gay green-and-white striped awnings. The Spanish Moroccan architectural style matched the new carousel building, which can still be seen at the old Park's location at 38th Avenue and Tennyson Street.

This phrase has represented Elitch Gardens for more than seventy-five years.

Elitch Gardens offered dancing lessons for Denver's youngsters in the Trocadero, and Mulvihill's afternoon Tea Dances were an immediate success. Admission was five cents, and a strict behavior code was always in effect—white gloves required. In fact, it was during this time that a popular young Denver belle was tapped on the shoulder and asked to leave the dance floor for dancing cheek-to-cheek—with her uncle! Her name was Mamie Doud, and she would soon meet and marry a young West Point graduate named Dwight David Eisenhower.

In 1924, John Mulvihill hired a young window dresser named Arnold Gurtler away from the Daniels & Fisher Company, one of Denver's

Elitch-Long Floral Company delivery truck

Elitch Gardens' greenhouses

The famous manicured & sculpted flower beds at Elitch Gardens

premier department stores. Mulvihill felt his ballroom had become so successful that it needed and deserved a complete facelift. Gurtler would undertake a complete renovation, beginning with a new floating dance floor, just like the one recently installed in the prestigious Antlers Hotel's ballroom in Colorado Springs. It was constructed of tongue-and-groove polished pine planks laid over thick square "springs" of woven horsehair. As they swayed to the music, the dancers indeed felt like they were floating!

The Theatre at the Gardens also flourished under John Mulvihill's guidance. He hired Rollo Lloyd as his director, followed by Melville

Entrance to the Trocadero at Elitch Gardens

The Trocadero Ballroom ☞ 1917–1975

Burke, and finally John Hayden. His stars during these years included, in 1922, a young Edward G. Robinson, whom Mulvihill constantly reprimanded for his "sloppy appearance." Beautiful Helen Menken (who would later marry an up-and-coming Humphrey Bogart) was his leading lady in both 1922 and 1924. Beulah Bondi starred in the productions of 1925 and 1926.

The 1926 season brought another leading man, Fredric March, to Denver. Mulvihill later liked to brag that he had hired the actor for a mere $60 a week, when just a few years later he would command the unheard-of price of $5,000 per week!

Fredric March starred in the Elitch Gardens Theatre during the 1926, 1927, and 1928 seasons. In 1926, he informed Mulvihill that he planned to marry his costar, Florence Eldridge. Mulvihill forbade it, and one evening after the performance, the two young lovers eloped to Colorado Springs, were married, and spent their wedding night at the Broadmoor Hotel. When they returned to the Gardens, Mulvihill promptly fired *her*! Incidentally, the couple remained happily married for over forty years until Eldridge's death.

Other stars appearing at the theater in those years were Sylvia Sydney in 1928 and George Brent and Victor Jory in 1929.

At the close of the 1929 season John Mulvihill realized the time had come to take stock. His health was not good, and he was aware this season would most likely be his last. But he also felt great satisfaction that his Park would enter the coming decade as a solvent and immensely successful enterprise. The Roaring Twenties had been an upward spiral of easy money and ceaseless partying all over the country, and in Denver, Elitch Gardens had become the center of the fun.

Edward G. Robinson ～ 1922

Fredric March
～ 1926–1928 leading man

Mulvihill was also pleased with his manager, young Arnold Gurtler, now married to his only child, Marie. His son-in-law had proven himself to be a loyal and invaluable assistant, so John knew all his years of long hours and hard work weren't in vain. His Park was in good hands.

Theater cast of 1926 with Fredric March as leading man and his future wife, Florence Eldridge, as leading lady

5

The Golden Era of the Park

JOHN MULVIHILL'S ELITCH GARDENS may have been in good economic shape at the start of the 1930s, but, in the big world outside the Park's elaborate stucco entrance gate, things were rapidly falling apart—the Great Depression had arrived.

Herbert Hoover was now president of the United States. The bright future and bold promises of just a few months previous were suddenly no more than so much dust in the wind. Worldwide political unrest was rampant, and both agriculture and industry were dangerously overexpanded. The increasing effectiveness of machinery had caused widespread unemployment, and credit had been stretched beyond the limit. International trade was badly out of balance, and the banking system was defective to its roots.

Colorado, due to its dependence on mining, suffered massive unemployment and a crippling business slowdown. By 1932, over forty thousand of its citizens had neither a job nor adequate food. Additionally, during the boom years of World War I, thousands of acres of prairie grassland had been plowed up to accommodate the demand for wheat. The ensuing years, however, brought low prices and dry times. Exposed topsoil blew into dark clouds of dust that stretched as far as the eye could see, choking the hope out of the farmers and ranchers of Colorado's eastern plains.

Things were certainly no better in Denver. Much of the large Slav population living in Globeville, which had mostly worked in the slaughterhouses at the nearby stockyards, was now idle, as were many of the more than eight thousand African Americans who had crowded into the city's Five Points area. There was a busy soup kitchen on Larimer Street, and World War I veterans were panhandling outside the Brown Palace Hotel.

Fortunately, Denverites were able to enjoy a brief respite when the price of gold rose once again to $35 an ounce, and there was a temporary resurgence of mining in the neighboring mountains.

Then, in 1933, Franklin D. Roosevelt was elected president and with the words "The only thing we have to fear is fear itself," enacted the New Deal for Relief and Recovery. In Colorado, scenic highways were built, historic attractions were constructed, public parks were created, and new agricultural experiments were undertaken. Mayor Robert Speer's new City and County Building was completed in 1933. To add to Coloradans' fragile hopes, molybdenum and vanadium, necessary for the manufacture of steel, had been newly discovered in the ore-rich mountains near Leadville.

John Mulvihill passed away in 1930, and his son-in-law, Arnold Gurtler, took over ownership of Elitch Gardens. Gurtler had grown up in Leadville. Most of his family worked in the silver and gold mines there. But early on, Arnold had made the decision that his future lay beyond the remote mountain town, so he moved to Denver. He found he had a talent for decorating, and was hired by the prestigious Daniels & Fisher Company on 16th Street as a window dresser. In the 1920s, the store's elaborate windows rivaled those of the largest department stores in Chicago and New York, and a good window dresser was an important employee.

When Gurtler was hired to decorate the Trocadero Ballroom, he met John Mulvihill's daughter, Marie. Immediately after they were married, the young couple moved into her family's home at 3814 Newton Street. A few years later, the entire family moved into a more impressive residence at 4209 West 38th Avenue, near Elitch Gardens.

Arnold and Marie would continue to live here until 1963. One lovely September afternoon in 1936, they hosted the widely attended society wedding of *Denver Post* heiress Helen Bonfils to Elitch Theatre director George Somnes in their rose garden.

Arnold Gurtler quickly set out to enact his own improvements to the Park. His new advertising stated, "Come to Elitch Gardens where a quarter can buy a day of dreams!"

One of his first improvements was to tear down the old wooden fence surrounding the Park, and replace it with a wire one that allowed passersby to see all the fun that beckoned from inside. He had finally closed Mary's zoo, and had given its two remaining residents—two very elderly bears—to the Denver Zoo. He filled in the famous bear pit in 1936, the same year he installed a new Ferris wheel nearby.

Realizing how much Denverites loved the Park's formal gardens, Gurtler expanded that portion of the operation and built additional greenhouses along 38th Avenue, where the last of the zoo enclosures had stood. He wisely hired George Gero as Elitch Gardens' head

Arnold Gurtler
President, Elitch Gardens
1930–1950

gardener. It was a perfect pairing. Gero set out more than 50,000 plantings each spring, and also instituted his popular "Dahlia Farm." The talented gardener gained a national reputation for his magnificent topiary creations. The most famous of these was his Floral Clock, which exhibited the time, day, month, and year in an ever-changing variety of greenery and blossoms. This much-beloved clock kept perfect time for over half a century. It only ceased to do so in 1995, when it was moved to the foot of the Ferris wheel at the Park's new location in central Denver. Unfortunately, no amount of care or adjustment could make it run again. Before the 1997 season began, the venerable old clock was permanently removed.

In 1938, Gurtler expanded Elitch Gardens' floral endeavor into the more aggressive and successful Park-Elitch Floral Company. Its motto was "Better Flowers Arranged Properly at Reasonable Prices for All Occasions." He even opened a branch at a downtown location in the Denver Dry Goods building.

There was no professional baseball in Denver in the 1930s, but semi-professional leagues were immensely popular. Gurtler reestablished and enlarged John Elitch's baseball field at the southwest corner of the Park. He built a large grandstand to accommodate the eager crowds. This was Denver's first organized baseball, and there were often three games daily. The M&O Cigar team was the perennial champion, but the Elitch Gardens team was lucky enough to capture several silver cups as well.

The greatest change that Arnold Gurtler made to Elitch Gardens concerned the Trocadero Ballroom. It had truly come into its own with the advent of the Great Depression and the newfound popularity of ballroom dancing. It was an affordable form of escape for beleaguered Americans.

Elitch Gardens' famous Floral Clock

Elitch Gardens' baseball team ✐ Batboys are Jack & Budd Gurtler

Gurtler elaborately decorated the cavernous facility—a 150-foot-long dance floor with wide, arched promenades on either side and an adjacent grille room—in a different theme each season, transforming it into a virtual fairyland. Bathed in bunting and a profusion of colored lights, it was ideal for its new role as "The Summer Home of the Big Band Sound."

Gurtler had become associated with a booking agency (eventually to become the mighty MCA—Music Corporation of America) that scheduled playing dates for all the most popular bands of the era. Of course, Elitch Gardens' Troc became a regular stop for them. Thus, the likes of the Dorseys, both Tommy and Jimmy; Harry James; Les Brown, accompanied by his young singer, Doris Day; Guy Lombardo; Stan Kenton; Buddy Rich; Tex Beneke; Wayne King; Gene Krupa; Lawrence Welk; Bob Crosby (Bing's younger brother); Ozzie Nelson with his singer Harriet Hilliard; Dick Jurgens; and Eddy Howard appeared each season.

Benny Goodman was hired to play the ballroom, but lasted only one night. He had decided to try out his new swing sound on the road, and his rapt Denver audience that evening preferred standing around the bandstand listening intently rather than dancing. Gurtler was *not* impressed, and promptly replaced the band with a local group. Benny Goodman went on to California and the rest is history. Afterward, he would refer to his sojourn at Elitch Gardens as "The Denver Blues."

Although he had sat in on a few jam sessions at the Troc when he was a student at the University of Colorado, Glenn Miller was perhaps the sole exception to the roster of prominent bandleaders who appeared at the ballroom. After his death in the Second World War, however, his band made regular appearances there.

Tommy Dorsey

Harry James

Les Brown

*Doris Day, singer with
Les Brown's Band of Renown*

Ozzie Nelson and his orchestra with his singer, Harriet Hilliard

Lawrence Welk and his orchestra

*Popular Eddy Howard
and his orchestra*

Dick Jurgens

Gurtler also began the tradition of "An Evening at the Troc," a radio program that was broadcast over KOA radio (in which Gurtler held a financial interest) every Saturday night for more than thirty years. The station's signal was so strong that the ballroom's music could be heard and enjoyed across most of the West and Southwest, which caused Elitch Gardens', and especially the Trocadero's, fame to spread. The adjacent Trocadero Court charged a dollar for table reservations for an entire evening, and the Grille Room, which joined the ballroom through numerous open arches, was a very popular gathering place to get a cold drink or just chat.

Arnold and Marie Gurtler enjoyed traveling to New York City each winter for the theater season, and would line up plays and book actors for their own theater's upcoming summer season. Gurtler kept a hand-written, looseleaf record of casting notes about each player he interviewed. One such entry read, "Don't interview again. Ears too big." That unfortunate actor's name was Clark Gable!

Stars who came to Elitch Gardens for a season during these years included Flobell Fairbanks (1931), who had been recommended by her uncle Douglas; Don Woods (1933), who began an association of many years, first as an actor and later as a director; Helen Bonfils (1934–1947), the prominent Denver socialite and owner of the *Denver Post* newspaper empire; and Jane Wyatt (1939), who would later be best known for her television role in *Father Knows Best*.

During this time the theater was fondly known as "the Playhouse in the Gardens." Performances were sold out long in advance, and usually for the entire season. Season tickets were passed down within families and often were listed in divorce settlements. In fact, one day the box

Guests enjoying Elitch Gardens ≈ *1930s*

office received a call. The caller said she had read in that morning's paper that Mrs. So-and-so had died. The caller knew the deceased had always had seats 1 and 2 in Row F, and she now wanted those tickets transferred to her name!

Mary Elitch, "The Gracious Lady of the Gardens," died of a massive heart attack in 1936 at the age of eighty. She was laid to rest next to her beloved John at Fairmont Cemetery. Her Last Will and Testament revealed an estate containing no real property. Her personal property, valued at $6,500 and meticulously listed, included her jewelry—a few diamonds, pearls, and a family cameo—her furs, several books, and paintings. Her beneficiaries were her sister, Anna Schilling, and Katherine Long, the daughter of her second husband, Thomas. She left her oriental rugs and furniture to charity, and her clothing to the costume department of the theater. Her collection of autographed photographs in the theater lobby went to John Mulvihill, and since he had preceded her in death, to Arnold Gurtler.

In the fifty-six years she had lived in Denver, Mary Elitch's dainty foot had made a deep and indelible imprint. She had stood on her own as a woman alone against nearly overpowering odds, and created in Elitch Gardens a successful major attraction in the western United States. In fact, in 1996, sixty years after her death, she was inducted into the Colorado Business Hall of Fame, where she was extolled as "dedicating her life to the success of the State of Colorado … exemplifying the type of leadership and commitment that have created visions for the future of Colorado."

The end of the 1930s brought the unsettling news of political unrest in Europe; but all that seemed very far away as Elitch Gardens celebrated

Mary Elitch Long
⌐ 1934

Mary's second house in the Gardens

its Golden Jubilee, or fiftieth anniversary of the theater, during the 1941 season. Both Colorado governor Ralph Carr and Denver mayor Ben Stapleton attended the opening festivities in May.

Then, that December, the unthinkable happened—America was at war. Rocky Mountain Arsenal, Lowry Airfield, Buckley Field, and the Denver Arms Camp (later to become the Federal Center) sprang up and brought to Denver thousands of new citizens and millions of dollars in federal money. To better serve this population boom, and as an answer to wartime gasoline shortages, the city renewed and expanded the nearly forgotten tramway system. Denver had suddenly become a crowded, bustling city in search of fun for its leisure time. And Elitch Gardens, conveniently on the tramway line, was ready and willing to provide it. Every man and woman in uniform was admitted to the Park and onto all rides free of charge during the war years.

The Park suffered its worst tragedy on July 16, 1944. Fire erupted in the Old Mill Tunnel of Love, trapping and burning alive six screaming souls. The old wooden tunnel had turned into a raging inferno by the time firemen arrived. Thick black smoke billowed to a height of over 150 feet in the air. It was out of control within minutes. No one knew what had caused it. There were no answers to the whispered questions of "Was the attraction safe?" and "Did people die needlessly after the fire was discovered?" and the most important one—"Why did it take so long to report the fire?"

The ensuing coroner's inquest lasted six hours and involved interviews with twenty-three witnesses. The 135-page report blamed the age of the attraction, ignorance, neglect, and carelessness. It seemed that fire engines were needlessly delayed by a locked gate. Only a single fire

The Old Mill fire ≈ *1944*

hydrant existed in the Park, forcing the majority of the hoses to be threaded in from 38th Avenue. Unfortunately, after that was done, it was discovered that the hoses weren't long enough to reach the site of the fire. Additionally, the regularly scheduled fire inspections proved to be no more than courtesy calls. As the result of all this, the city of Denver enacted a fire code that has been in effect ever since.

The irony of this fire was that it had occurred on the exact same site of the terrible fire of 1914. The big difference this time, however, was the unforgettable sight of those six dead bodies lying in a row under sheets in the blackened grass. Gurtler would hear their screams until the day he died.

Jack Gurtler, left, and Budd Gurtler, right, copresidents of Elitch Gardens

Arnold Gurtler's sons, Jack and Budd, had joined the Marines to fight for their country. At the end of the war in 1945, they returned to Elitch Gardens. They had worked at various jobs throughout the Park since their boyhoods—ushers in the theater, parking lot attendants, grunt labor in the greenhouses and all around the grounds—so they were now well prepared to take their places on the management team. The two brothers decided to alternate seasons managing the theater and the Trocadero in order to gain experience in both. They made it a priority to continually upgrade and adapt Elitch Gardens' attractions to match the tempo of the times.

A scene in Elitch Gardens' KiddieLand

Jack and Budd Gurtler were a perfect balance as partners, even though they were nearly complete opposites in all ways. Physically, Budd was tall and slender, while Jack was of a sturdier build, even heavy in his later years. Budd was the quieter, more serious brother who excelled in business planning, while Jack was the gregarious, hail-fellow-well-met who was perfect in the public relations role of the Park's management.

Their first innovation was KiddieLand. A small play area had existed at the Park since its opening day, but through the years, it served merely as a convenience for harried mothers. Even Mary Elitch's petting zoo had been phased out long ago. Interestingly enough, popular amusement parks across the nation had always catered to the enjoyment of

Hopalong Cassidy greets guests at the grand opening of KiddieLand

adults—and Elitch Gardens was no exception. The rides were full-sized; the Orchard Café offered the finest food and libation; the theater offered sophisticated productions; and romance bloomed nightly at the Trocadero Ballroom. However, the baby boom of the 1940s changed all that. Jack and Budd Gurtler were actually quite savvy to create a section of Elitch Gardens where all the rides were scaled to small children.

Popular Hollywood cowboy star Hopalong Cassidy welcomed a record crowd of young Denverites on opening day in 1952. Elitch Gardens' KiddieLand had a storybook theme, and was highlighted once again by a petting zoo, featuring Mary's little lamb, the three little pigs, and the three billy goats gruff, to mention only a few. The refreshment stand at KiddieLand was excavated to allow the employees to stand below ground level and serve their little customers at eye level.

In 1950, the Gurtler brothers developed an area of the Park called Fryer's Hill, which contained pathways and game booths and was named after a silver-producing hill in their father's native Leadville.

Hollywood began filming *The Glenn Miller Story*, starring Jimmy Stewart and June Allison, in 1954, and the Trocadero Ballroom was used as a location for several scenes. Airmen stationed at Lowry Airfield served as extras in the movie. The Gurtler family invited Miller's sister, who lived in Greeley at the time, to watch the production.

Budd Gurtler took a special interest in the Park-Elitch Floral Company. Under his guidance, Elitch Gardens became the largest supplier of carnations in the country, selling and shipping 750,000 blooms annually. In the early 1950s, the Park had six hundred employees in the greenhouses alone. Budd was a founding member of the Colorado Carnation Growers Association, and initiated the process of dying white carnations various colors to match special occasions, as well as matching an entire generation of young ladies' prom gowns. Budd also invented the peppermint carnation.

In 1955, the concept of amusement parks changed forever with the opening of Walt Disney's Disneyland, in California. It was billed from the beginning as entertainment for both adults and children, and set out to educate its guests as well as to thrill them with the usual rides and attractions. Disneyland encompassed several smaller theme parks—Tomorrowland, reminiscent of a World's Fair of the future;

Frontierland, accenting America's history; and Fantasyland, which featured some of America's favorite fairy tales. These were all grouped around Main Street, built to resemble a turn-of-the-century street in a small town, and to evoke an idealized past that people found appealing. Disneyland became a symbol of American hopefulness and optimism, drawing an astounding one million visitors in less than two months of operation, and over four million in its inaugural year.

Walt Disney advertised his new theme park regularly on his weekly television program, and suddenly the thought of visiting, if not Disneyland, the nearest amusement park was on everybody's mind. Naturally, this put a new emphasis and added pressure on every amusement park across the country. And Elitch Gardens was no exception.

In 1958, Elitch Gardens' Greek Revival stucco gate, which had become a Denver landmark, had to be torn down to facilitate the widening of 38th Avenue. Letters to the editor protesting the demolition filled the newspapers of the day. Denverites felt very possessive of what they thought of as *their* amusement park. Arnold Gurtler often reminisced about walking to that gate, which stood majestically at the end of the 38th Avenue trolley line, and watching all the eager families disembark carrying wicker picnic baskets. The small band of musicians stationed in the big gate's loft struck up a merry tune with the arrival of each trolley to welcome guests into the Park.

After Arnold Gurtler turned the management of his Park over to his sons, he would stroll in after supper on those long summer evenings and sit in one of the metal chairs arranged under the big shade trees outside the theater. There, he would hold court, asking first one person to sit down and chat for a bit and then another. Passersby were expected to wait for that coveted invitation, of course; a stern glance discouraged anyone else.

According to his family, Arnold's legacy to Elitch Gardens was his commitment to encouraging his employees, as well as his grandchildren, to strive to become the best people they possibly could. It was almost as if his credo was "I was given a chance (to get out of the mines of Leadville as a boy and better myself), and I believe everybody deserves one too."

For countless Denver kids, Elitch Gardens, one of the largest employers of youth in Colorado, was their first job experience. For many, lifelong friendships, romances, and marriages were formed at the Park. Parents were pleased that Elitch's always insisted upon the highest standards in dress and behavior and instilled a work ethic that would benefit these young people throughout their lives—values like honesty, promptness, cleanliness, patience, and courtesy. Elitch Gardens hired around eleven hundred kids each summer at their old location and currently hire nearly double that number at the new.

The Theatre at the Gardens was also at its zenith during these golden years. Handsome Raymond Burr led the 1944 theater company, and Patricia Neal was the leading lady of 1947. In 1951, a shy, young ingénue from the East arrived and rented a basement room at 4020 Raleigh Street (39th and Tennyson). She hung her laundry under the big trees in the backyard, and rode a borrowed bicycle to rehearsals each day. She was cooperative, hardworking, and a very popular member of the company. This lovely lady would go on to become an Oscar-winning actress, and then acquire the title Her Serene Highness, the Princess of Monaco. Her name was Grace Kelly. Popular actor Wendell Cory rounded out the decade as leading man in 1959.

Theater cast of 1944 with Raymond Burr as leading man

Patricia Neal ❧ 1947

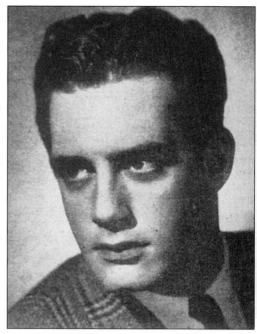

Raymond Burr ❧ 1944

Her Serene Highness, Princess Grace of Monaco
née Grace Kelly ☞ 1951

Theater cast of 1951. Grace Kelly is at the far left.
Gurtler had a long-standing joke of having whoever stood at the far left in a photoshoot
beat the slow-devleoping camera to leisurely pose on the right side of the photo.

Helen Bonfils, actress &
manager of the Theatre
at the Gardens
☞ 1934–1954

The Elitch Gardens' ushers ☞ c. 1930
See arrows—Jack Gurtler, left; Budd Gurtler, right

The lobby of the theater filled with autographed photographs of past players

6

The Sixties and Beyond

SIMPLY PUT, AMERICA, as if it were on a giant roller coaster ride, turned upside down and inside out in the sixties. The previous decade had seen the population shift from a rural to an urban society, and then suburban society. The postwar economic boom had raised the entire country's standard of living.

The Innovator, who had always characterized America's progress, was now replaced by the Marketer. In 1957, Sputnik brought on a space race with our Cold War enemy, the Soviet Union, which in turn accented an image of American complacency and material self-indulgence.

A youthful and vital John Fitzgerald Kennedy was elected president in 1960 and challenged every citizen to change that image. And change we did. Events—the Civil Rights Movement, the Cuban Missile Crisis, the Vietnam War, the Berlin Wall—were happening quickly, one upon the other, and creating drastic social changes that would manifest themselves in a rebellion of America's youth unlike anything that had ever come before or since.

The sixties will be remembered as a decade of crisis, conflict, and turmoil. It was as if our whole country were undergoing a nervous breakdown of sorts—a decade of causes that began in hope and ended in despair, a decade that would contain both the nonviolent vision of Martin Luther King, Jr., and the angry defiance of Malcolm X; the liberalism of Eugene McCarthy and the bigotry of George Wallace; the altruistic youth of the Peace Corps and the angry violence of the antiwar demonstrations; and the simple optimistic phrases of the Kingston Trio and the biting words of Bob Dylan.

Traditional values were helplessly trampled in the wake of a new sexual freedom and the widespread use of drugs. By the middle of the decade, more young people than ever before were enrolled in our colleges, and yet those same campuses were in revolt. America was at war with itself—a generational war, one of parent against child.

Our heroes were being killed—John Kennedy, Martin Luther King, Jr., and Bobby Kennedy—all brutally assassinated before our eyes on family television screens. Malcolm X was gunned down in his prime. As one might imagine, there was little inclination in these tumultuous times for a leisurely afternoon spent at an amusement park. Then, in 1969, just as Charles Lindbergh's lonely flight across the ocean had provided a balm to heal the craziness of the twenties, Neil Armstrong's first footprint upon the moon's surface unified America. It was almost as if the nation had found itself once again in the promise of the future.

But we would never be the same. And to gain and keep the attention of this new breed of visitor, amusement rides and attractions had to deliver greater thrills than ever before. Jack and Budd Gurtler well understood this.

The aluminum Elitch Gardens' entrance gate ⌒ 1959–1994

The Gurtler brothers knew they had to make some drastic changes to the Park. They made the determination to look forward and not backward, and in 1960 demolished Mary Elitch's house. Their greatest project was Mister Twister, a ninety-six-foot-tall wooden roller coaster that was advertised as "three-quarters of a mile of turning, churning torture." The Twister opened in 1965, and was always included in the list of the top ten in the country by coaster buffs. Designed by John Allen, it was considered to be the grandest roller coaster of the century. Mister Twister contained an eighty-foot drop, two 360-degree turns, a double helix, and a tunnel. It was truly state-of-the-art, and was instantly a hit.

"Mister Twister" ~ 1965–1994

In order to accommodate the need for additional parking, Budd reluctantly agreed to raze the greenhouses along 38th Avenue.

Due to the urging of longtime Park publicist John Eby, Jack and Budd built a miniature golf course in what remained of Mary Elitch's apple orchard. They instituted The Elitch Invitational Golf Tournament, with Denver's prominent businessmen as well as theater stars as participants. This popular annual event would, over the next ten years, raise an impressive $43,000 for scholarships.

The Splinter, a flume ride (where one sits in a hollowed-out log and rides down a water-filled chute), premiered in 1978. The Gurtlers insisted it be built around and through their grandfather Mulvihill's Wildcat Coaster ride in order to preserve this piece of Elitch Gardens' rich history.

"The Splinter" ⌒ *1978–1994*

Jack Gurtler, left; Arnold Gurtler, center; Budd Gurtler, right

The Trocadero Ballroom comes down ⌒ 1975

The sixties also brought a decline in the popularity of ballroom dancing; young people much preferred rock concerts. Also, bands were no
longer willing to embark on long road trips. For Elitch's, the Trocadero
had become a drafty dinosaur. In 1975, Jack and Budd were forced to
make the *very* difficult decision to tear it down. They had discussed this
on and off for four years; Budd had nursed the fading hope that dancing

to live bands would make a comeback. When they announced their plans, there arose such a public outcry that the Park's switchboard was burdened with complaints for over a week. "Where was their support when we needed it?" the brothers lamented.

Jack Gurtler, in particular, often waxed nostalgic about the old ballroom. He would recount that throughout its history, dancing lessons—tap, ballroom, as well as ballet—were offered to Denver's preteens and teens. However, like many boys his age, young Jack was seldom to be found whenever his lessons were scheduled.

"Well," he said, "my first 'real date' happened to be at the Troc and sure enough I clumsily walked all over my young lady's feet for most of the evening. Needless to say, there wasn't a second date!"

Jack must have learned something, however, for in later years he often told of courting his wife to the music of Dick Jurgens and Les Brown.

Wayne King and his orchestra, an old favorite, were invited to play to an overflowing crowd for the last Saturday evening performance.

The only survivors of the Trocadero are several small tables. The tables, the tops of which were constructed of pieces of the ballroom's floor, are still in use at Mulvihill's Sports Bar at Six Flags Elitch Gardens. The light, which was suspended in the middle of the ballroom and indicated what kind of dance—fox-trot, waltz, or two-step—was coming up, is now used only for special occasions. But the music and the memories live on.

With the burgeoning popularity of television, the Theatre at the Gardens also was forced to make some drastic changes. In 1963, a switch was made from sixty-three years of summer stock to very successful star-centered performances. The roll call of stars to play at Elitch's for a week or two, often returning for a second or third subsequent engagement, reads like a Who's Who from both cinema and television.

The last production of the theater occurred in 1991, ending a treasured Denver tradition that had endured for one hundred years.

Cloris Leachman as Grandma Moses ☞ *1982*

Roll Call of Stars from 1963 to the close of the theater

Joe E. Brown, 1963
Walter Pidgeon, 1964
Peggy Cass, 1964
James Coco, 1964
Darren McGavin, 1964
Roger Smith, 1964
  (TV actor & husband of
  Ann-Margret)
Cesar Romero, 1964

Christina Crawford, 1964
  (daughter of Joan Crawford
  & author of best-selling
  Mommie Dearest)
Barbara Bel Geddes, 1964
Marjorie Lord, 1964
Cornelia Otis Skinner, 1964
Hal March, 1964; 1965
Arlene Francis, 1964; 1965; 1969

Eve Arden, 1965
Kathy Nolan, 1965
Vivian Vance, 1965
Hermione Gingold, 1965
Ralph Meeker, 1965
Marisa Pavan, 1965
Kitty Carlisle, 1965; 1970
Tom Ewell, 1966; 1969
Cliff Arquette, 1966
Gloria Swanson, 1967
Joan Fontaine, 1968
Forrest Tucker, 1968
Kathryn Crosby, 1968
   (wife of Bing Crosby)
Morey Amsterdam, 1968
Dick Van Patten, 1968
Robert Cummings, 1968
Shirley Booth, 1968
Ann Sothern, 1968
Barry Nelson, 1968; 1969; 1971
James Whitmore, 1969
Tom Poston, 1969
Myrna Loy, 1969
George Grizzard, 1969
Noel Harrison, 1970; 1982
   (son of Rex Harrison)
George Gobel, 1971
Douglas Fairbanks, Jr., 1971; 1973
Farley Granger, 1971
Sid Caesar, 1971; 1974
Edie Adams, 1971
Mickey Rooney, 1972; 1974
Brandon de Wilde, 1972
   (de Wilde was killed in an
   automobile accident in
   neighboring Lakewood
   during the season)

Maureen O'Sullivan, 1972; 1982;
   1983
Barbara Rush, 1972
Jose Ferrer, 1973
Gig Young, 1973
Shelley Winters, 1973; 1983
John Astin, 1973; 1974
Patty Duke, 1973; 1974
Sandy Dennis, 1974
Steve Allen & Jayne Meadows,
   1974
Gary Merrill, 1974
Kim Hunter, 1975
Edward Mulhare, 1975
Lynn Redgrave, 1975
Ginger Rogers, 1975
Betsy Palmer, 1975
William Shatner, 1975
David McCallum, 1976; 1982; 1983
Lana Turner, 1977
John Raitt, 1977; 1979
   (father of singer Bonnie Raitt)
Van Johnson, 1977
Keir Dullea, 1977; 1982; 1983
Julie Harris, 1978
Pat O'Brien, 1979
Cloris Leachman, 1982; 1983
Richard Kiley, 1982; 1983
Tyrone Power III, 1982; 1983
   (son of movie star Tyrone Power)
Gabe Kaplan, 1982; 1983
Tammy Grimes, 1982; 1983
Margaret Whiting, 1985
Pat Hinkle, 1987
Nancy Walker, 1987

Walter Pidgeon ☞ *1964*

Myrna Loy ☞ *1969*

Douglas Fairbanks, Jr., looking at the autographed photo of his father in the theater lobby
☞ *1971*

Bob Cummings ☞ *1968*

7

The End of an Era

JACK AND BUDD GURTLER continued to make changes to the Park to match the public's ever-evolving tastes, even to the point of hosting blockbuster pop concerts that included stars all the way from Victor Borge and Ray Charles to Kris Kristofferson and the Nitty Gritty Dirt Band.

In 1985, Sandy Gurtler, Budd's son, took the helm of Elitch Gardens. He was the fourth generation of the Mulvihill-Gurtler family to do so. Like his uncle and his father before him, he had worked in the Park since he was a boy, and like them, he had mastered every aspect of its management. Jack Gurtler had retired in 1979, and he died in 1993. Budd died in 1992. Before his death, Budd was asked what had been his favorite part of Elitch Gardens during his fifty-six-year association with the Park.

"The noise, and the lights, but mostly the children's laughter," he reminisced.

Years later, Sandy would speak fondly of the frequent family dinners of his childhood, presided over by his grandfather, Arnold. Both his

Sandy Gurtler, president of Elitch Gardens
1985–1996

uncle Jack's and his father's families were expected to be present. These dinners took place at either son's home, or often at the Orchard Café at the Park. The family business was always the topic of discussion. The two young grandsons, Sandy and his cousin John were expected to listen and participate. This was how they learned the amusement park business inside and out, and also a deep-rooted family philosophy.

Sandy's first challenge was to carry out the family's long-range plans to move Elitch Gardens to a more central location. There were several reasons necessitating this. The Park had reached its limit—it simply had no more room to expand. As new rides were acquired, they even had to be placed on top of one another. For example, the new Spider ride was constructed atop the bumper-car building. Also, the Gardens' family appeal had waned in favor of a new breed of thrill-seeking teenagers. And finally, tourists, quickly becoming the lifeblood of the amusement industry, were unwilling to travel to northwest Denver to search the Park out.

The Gurtlers believed Elitch Gardens was a rich blend of history, community involvement, and wholesome family entertainment in Denver, and they were committed to keeping it the first-class, family-oriented Park it always had been. In more recent years, as space became more and more of a premium and bigger, newer rides became necessary, Elitch's flower gardens shrank. "This is Elitch Gardens," Budd Gurtler complained, "Not Elitch asphalt!" He dreamed of a cutting-edge amusement park—the very latest rides sprinkled among lush flower gardens—with plenty of parking.

So, the move had to take place. The family carefully considered several sites. Then, in 1989, Denver voters approved $14 million worth of bond subsidies for floodplain and road improvements in an area of lower downtown in the Central Platte River Valley. The city had ambitious plans for a complete revitalization of this area, adjacent to the popular Mile High Football Stadium. The plans included a world-class baseball park, a new basketball/hockey/concert arena, and a state-of-the-art aquarium—a perfect place for Elitch Gardens Amusement Park. Further, city officials enticed the Gurtler family with a promise of $21 million in public funds to help offset their cleanup and construction costs.

It wasn't an easy sell! The neglected, treeless, sixty-eight-acre lot, termed a Superfund site by the Environmental Protection Agency, had

The "new" Elitch Gardens' location—a first look ➣ 1993

been used as a railroad yard for over a hundred years. It was covered with contaminated soil that had been long and thoroughly saturated with spilled kerosene, oil, and coal. Even the hardiest weed had a tough time taking root there. In recent years, the land had become the home of vagrants, vandals, and large river rats.

One certainly had to admire Sandy Gurtler's powers of imagination. He only had to close his eyes to envision all the latest rides surrounded by 84,000 square feet of groomed and blooming gardens; 3,000 tall shade-providing trees; and even, as a tribute to Mary Elitch herself, a rose, herb, and vegetable garden. But would the generations of people who had grown up under the spreading branches of the trees at the old Elitch Gardens share his vision? The downside was all too clear. But there was an upside too—the influx of substantial funds, the convenient location near downtown Denver, and easy access to Denver's primary interstate highway.

By 1994, the $95 million financing package was finalized. Gurtler, lacking the necessary investment capital, formed several limited partnerships to make this happen (a move that would later come back to haunt him).

And so construction began. To begin with, the contaminated soil had to be scraped away and hauled off so that truckload after truckload of good soil could be brought in; hundreds of saplings were planted and thousands of fragile flowers were arranged, row upon row, in neat beds.

The new Elitch Gardens opened in May 1995. Fifteen of its eighteen major rides had been brought from the old location. The centerpiece of the Park was Twister II, a wooden roller coaster whose blueprint was taken from the original Mister Twister. The popular Sidewinder Coaster and the old Ferris wheel were also relocated.

Elitch Gardens' most venerable attraction, its 1928 PTC #51 carousel, was dismantled, stripped, repaired, and painted. It was moved to the new park and placed in a building reminiscent of its original yellow stucco home. It was given a new oak and walnut floor, which was left beautifully natural. An amazing seven pounds of nails, screws, rivets, and metal fasteners that had been used in various repairs over the years were removed during the record four-and-a-half-month restoration. In all, the new Elitch Gardens offered thirty-four rides and thirty-one games.

Elitch Gardens in its new home

Elitch Gardens was to become the cornerstone of Denver's Central Platte Valley Redevelopment project. By the millennium, visitors would enjoy Invesco Field at Mile High (Broncos football), Coors Field (Rockies baseball), the Pepsi Center (Nuggets basketball/Avalanche hockey/concert venue), Ocean Journey (aquarium), and an expanded Auraria Campus for Higher Education (containing the University of Colorado at Denver, Community College of Denver, and Metro State College of Colorado). All of these would be easily accessible via light rail and bus. The project was indeed a success.

But Denverites were shocked at their "new and improved" Elitch Gardens. As luck would have it, at least 94 of the 160 operating days that first season were rained out. The Park was under constant threat of flooding. "Well," everyone grumbled, "we shouldn't rush to judge. After all, it's only one season. Next year, everything will be just like it always was."

Unfortunately, the new park's second season proved to be nearly as disastrous. Nineteen ninety-six was an extremely hot summer, and shade from those struggling rain-soaked saplings was virtually nonexistent. Visitors, who had withheld their final judgment the previous season,

The "new" Elitch Gardens water park

now came with even higher expectations and wilted in long waiting lines under the summer sun, then left disgusted. It just didn't look or feel anything like the Park they grew up in. Where were the big old trees? Where was the shady picnic ground? And what happened to the admission price they remembered? They ignored all the touches intended to remind them of Elitch's rich heritage. There was the new Trocadero Theatre, whose façade was reminiscent of the Greek Revival, stucco entrance gate that had greeted them for so many years. The new theater paid homage to both the famous Trocadero Ballroom and the Theatre at the Gardens, in that it was built for use as a theater, and with the removal of its seven hundred seats, also as a dance floor. Further, its lobby was decorated with historic photos of the heyday of both the Elitch Theatre and the Troc. Nor did they seem to appreciate Miss Mary's Ice Cream & Sandwich Shoppe, John's Haberdashery & Gift Shoppe, Tortoni's Pizza Parlor, The Orchard Café, or J. M. Mulvihill's Sports Bar (the latter two also exhibiting historic photos). "What a disappointment!" they said. And unfortunately, the press agreed.

So, the verdict was in. The good people of Denver stayed away in droves. Then, when Gurtler's new partners began to pressure him for their money, he unsuccessfully pleaded for time—time to let the Park's trees mature and for Denverites to get used to its new features. But they refused.

The unthinkable was happening. Sandy Gurtler's options first narrowed and then were exhausted. He would be forced to sell Elitch Gardens, his family's business for four generations, in order to satisfy creditors who neither understood nor cared about the peculiarities of the amusement park business.

It was ironic, really. Mary Elitch had been forced to sell her beloved Gardens to a stranger exactly eighty years earlier because *she* was unable to pay her bills, and now history was repeating itself.

In 1996, Premier Parks, Inc., a publicly owned company that at the time operated twelve successful amusement parks across the country, purchased Elitch Gardens for $62.5 million. Premier immediately added $25 million worth of new rides and attractions, highlighted by a ten-acre water park.

In response to visitors' primary complaint, they even imported a type of fast-growing tree from Australia to help provide shade. As a result, the people of Denver seemed to slowly accept the new, new Elitch Gardens.

8

Into a Second Century

IN 1998, PREMIER PARKS, INC., purchased all of the Six Flags Amusement Parks—a total of thirty-nine theme and water parks throughout North America, Latin America, and Europe—for the sum of $2 billion. Six Flags' parks serve twenty of the twenty-five largest metropolitan areas in the United States, and annually serve more than fifty million guests worldwide. Six Flags also purchased the right to feature popular Warner Brothers and DC comic characters, who have become favorite figures to the Park's youngest visitors. From the beginning, however, corporate management stated their intention to retain the Elitch name.

"We are mindful of Elitch Gardens' rich history, and we do not want to forsake its legacy and what that legacy has meant to the community. We can't recreate the old Park, but we can try to recapture the feel of what made Elitch Gardens magic."

And so, Six Flags Elitch Gardens was born. Actually, it was a good fit, since the flags of six governments have flown over the land upon which the Park stands, each representing an important part of Colorado's history and rich heritage. First, in 1706, the ground was claimed by Spain, whose men had come grabbing gold with one hand while spreading Christianity with the other. In 1763, France claimed the area after French fur trappers followed the nearby Platte (French for "flat") River westward. Then, when Emperor Napoleon needed money to finance his European wars, he sold this land to U.S. president Thomas Jefferson in 1803.

In 1821, Mexico claimed that Spain had never agreed to cede the land to France, and since they (Mexico) had recently gained their independence from Spain and retaken all their holdings, the area now belonged to them. When Texas, in its turn, won independence from Mexico in 1836, Texans claimed this ground as part of their new Republic.

And finally, the land upon which Six Flags Elitch Gardens now stands became part of the newly formed state of Colorado (from a Spanish phrase meaning "reddish color") in 1876.

The corporation immediately invested $7.5 million in the Park to bring it up to Six Flags' standards and continue to add the latest thrill ride each season, thus remaining at the cutting edge of the industry.

So, Six Flags Elitch Gardens eagerly looks forward to welcoming guests into their second century, committed to maintaining the high standards set by John and Mary Elitch all those years ago. The Park remains a place for fun, a place for friends and family, and a place where dreams come true—if only for a day.

And what has become of the old Park site at 38th Avenue and Tennyson Street in northwest Denver? The thirty-two acres have become Highlands Garden Village, a $50 million development containing senior

Six Flags Elitch Gardens, entrance ⌁ 2000

apartments; single-family homes featuring garages that face alleys, big front porches, and broad sidewalks; townhomes; apartments; small businesses with living units built over them; a day care center, and a preschool. The concept behind the village is to create an old-fashioned, close-knit neighborhood more friendly to pedestrians than to car traffic. One of the new owners, Chuck Perry, grew up in Denver—he even worked as an usher in Elitch Gardens' Theatre as a boy. His wife also owns a popular North Denver restaurant.

Highlands Garden Village is a success. The developers have made an effort to honor the rich history of the property they occupy. Historic

Elitch Gardens photographs decorate the halls of the senior apartments, and the yellow stucco Spanish Moroccan-style carousel building remains. It is now used for public meetings, farmers' markets, and band concerts. Although the famous arched entrance gate is gone, Mary Elitch's original apple orchard has been replanted and remains as a greenbelt.

The venerable old Theatre at the Gardens still stands as well. It has been granted a National Historic Landmark status, sought by Budd Gurtler, as "The Oldest Summer Stock Theatre in America." Its new owners hope to follow through with his dreams to restore it for use as a community theater. Budd always thought it belonged in downtown Denver as part of the Denver Center for the Performing Arts.

And finally, pieces of wood from the old Mister Twister have been fashioned into nostalgic sidewalk sculpture, planters, and benches along Tennyson Street in the Park's old neighborhood.

Epilogue ⁓

The Legend of
Mary Elitch's Ghost

ON JULY 17, 1996, exactly sixty years to within a day after Mary Elitch's death (July 16, 1936), the final papers were signed between the Gurtler family and Perry Affordable Housing for the thirty-two-acre property that had been Martha and William Chilcott's farm, and then the site of so many of Mary Elitch's dreams and memories.

That July morning was one of those sparklingly beautiful Colorado summer days, and when Sandy Gurtler and his wife, Shirley, strolled the deserted grounds one last time, they beheld a startling sight. Sandy's mind was on the task that lay ahead—the final dismantling of his family's Park—and he gave no importance to the find. But Shirley immediately called me. When I arrived, the two of us stared silently and then exchanged knowing glances. Before us, an enormous maple tree that had shaded a side entrance of the theater for many, many years had mysteriously sheared off, a full five feet off the ground—there had been no storm the previous night, nor any wind—yet the old tree was cut completely in half, almost as if someone had taken an axe to its massive trunk. The tree had smashed into the adjacent deserted administration building, badly damaging a portion of a sturdy brick wall. We both shuddered in relief, for if it had chanced to fall the other way, it would have destroyed a wall of the venerable old theater like a stack of toothpicks. Shirley and I both knew what the other was thinking. Had Mary Elitch done this as a final act of disapproval? Was she making one final protest against the loss of her beloved park?

Almost immediately after Mary Elitch's death, the employees' stories of encounters with her ghost began, and they have continued over the years. The sightings usually take place in the theater, with Mary clad in a beautiful Victorian dress, wearing one of the large hats she loved. She usually speaks to the witness, and, with a few exceptions, the experience has never been reported as a bad or scary one.

I only half-believed all these stories until I had my own personal encounter. I never saw anything or heard anything unusual. In my case, I *felt* something. One afternoon, in my role as the Park archivist/historian, I was working alone in the theater, removing the historic photos from the walls of the dress circle. Each time I had an armful, I carried them down the left aisle to the stage, where I placed them in boxes to be later transferred to the Park's newly formed archives collection. I remember that I was thinking about nothing in particular, when suddenly it was as though I had run into a very solid, soft, warm wall. I couldn't move forward! It was almost as though someone were hugging me. Then, after a moment or two, it was gone and, nonplussed, I proceeded to the stage with my load. The amazing thing was that I felt no fear. It wasn't until later that I learned my encounter had taken place just below Mary Elitch's theater box.

Whenever I think of it, I like to believe that if indeed that *was* Mary Elitch's ghost, she approved of what I was doing and was trying to convey that to me. And if Mary's ghost is still out there at the old Park site, I picture her strolling around her Elitch Gardens on a soft summer night, stopping to listen to the carousel's band organ or the delighted screams of riders on the Wildcat or Mister Twister, or to bits of dialogue wafting through the open doorways of the theater. And I picture her smiling …

Chronology

1890 Elitch Gardens first opens its gates to the public. (The bustling little town of Denver was just thirty years old when Elitch's first opened.) John and Mary Elitch turned their farm in Denver's outlying Highlands area, complete with a small lake and an apple orchard, into a cool green oasis and a zoological park for all of Denver to enjoy.

1891 John Elitch dies. Mary continues to run Elitch Gardens and gains the distinction of being the only woman in the world to own and manage a successful summer resort. She was known throughout her life as "the Gracious Lady of the Gardens," and lived on the grounds until her death.

1891 The Elitch Gardens Playhouse (later Theatre) opens and begins its tradition of a century of first-class entertainment.

1897 The Elitch Gardens Theatre changes from vaudeville to legitimate theater. Early in the new century it featured such actors as Sarah Bernhardt, Douglas Fairbanks, Sr., and a young Cecil B. DeMille. In its middle years, Edward G. Robinson and Fredric March were the most prominent stars to begin their careers at Elitch's. Stars to appear at the theater during the 1940s were Raymond Burr and Patricia Neal. And in 1951, Grace Kelly was an unknown ingénue at Elitch Gardens. In the 1960s, the summer stock system gave way to star-centered productions, and many television and movie personalities of that era acted in the historic theater, including Lana Turner, Walter Pidgeon, Shelley Winters, Mickey Rooney, Patty Duke, and William Shatner. The Theatre at the Gardens has the distinction of being "The Oldest Summer Stock Theater in the United States."

1909   The log entrance gate is torn down and an ornate, Greek Revival–style stucco gate is built.

1916   Denver businessman John Mulvihill purchases Elitch Gardens from Mary Elitch, and begins a dynasty of four generations of family ownership.

1917   The Trocadero Ballroom opens. During the Big Band era, such famous bands as those of Tommy and Jimmy Dorsey; Benny Goodman; Guy Lombardo; Les Brown and his young singer, Doris Day; Harry James; Gene Krupa; Ozzie Nelson with his singer Harriet Hilliard; Lawrence Welk; Dick Jurgens; and Eddy Howard appeared regularly.

1922   The Wildcat Coaster is built. "Twist his Tail and Hear him Roar" read the advertisements of the day. The popular attraction was expanded in 1936.

1928   The carousel, which took master craftsmen three years to carve by hand, is delivered from the Philadelphia Toboggan Company. It is truly a survivor of an endangered species and operates in the Park today.

1930   John Mulvihill dies and his son-in-law, Arnold Gurtler, assumes ownership of Elitch Gardens.

1936 Mary Elitch dies.

1936 The Ferris wheel is erected. It was moved to the new Park location in 1994 and still operates there today.

1945 Jack and Budd Gurtler, Arnold's sons, return from service in World War II to take their places in the management of the Park.

1954 KiddieLand, conceived by Jack and Budd, opens. Popular television star Hopalong Cassidy presides over the opening ceremonies.

1958 The stucco entrance gate is torn down due to the widening of 38th Avenue. It is replaced by an Art Deco aluminum arch.

1965 The famous Mister Twister roller coaster is built and advertised "not to have a foot of straight track in it." It was torn down in 1994 when Elitch Gardens moved to its new location near downtown Denver.

1975 The famous Trocadero Ballroom is torn down. Ballroom dancing had been replaced by rock concerts and remaining Big Bands were no longer willing to undergo long road trips.

1985 Sandy Gurtler, great-grandson of John Mulvihill and son of Budd Gurtler, becomes president of Elitch Gardens.

1989 Denver voters approve $14 million in bond subsidies for floodplain and road improvements, enticing Elitch's to move the Park to a central Denver site.

1994 The final $95 million financing package is completed and construction begins on the new Elitch Gardens in the Central Platte River Valley near downtown Denver. It becomes the first amusement park to be built in an urban area in the United States in more than 30 years. After 104 years of successful operation, Elitch Gardens closes its doors forever at its famous northwest

Denver location. That location has since become a successful housing development.

1995 The new Elitch Gardens opens at its new location in central Denver.

1996 Premier Parks, Inc., a publicly held company, purchases Elitch Gardens and adds millions of dollars' worth of new rides and attractions.

1998 Premier Parks, Inc., acquires all of the Six Flags Amusement Parks worldwide, and Six Flags Elitch Gardens is born.

A Note on Sources

SEVERAL BOOKS were helpful in finding information about Denver's rich history, especially the following:

Arps, Laura Ward. *Denver in Slices*. Denver: Sage Books, 1959.

Brenneman, Bill. *Miracle on Cherry Creek*. Denver: World Press, Inc., 1973.

Muntz, Geoffrey, and Alan S. Wuth. *A Path Through Time: A Guide to the Platte River Greenway*. Frederick: Platte 'N Press Books, 1983.

Noel, Thomas. *Denver's Larimer Street: Main Street, Skid Row & Urban Renaissance*. Denver: Historic Denver, Inc., 1981.

Smiley, Jerome. *History of Denver*. Denver: Times-Sun Publishing, 1901.

Turk, Gayle. *Trial & Triumph: Quick History of Denver*. Colorado Springs: Little London Press, 1978.

Index ⤳